A Taste of Woodland

Recipes from Woodland, the Community Church
Bradenton, Florida

Lakewood Ranch, Florida

From Our Pastor

Do you like to eat? I know, a ridiculous question – right? Maybe a better question is – "What's your favorite food?" The people of Woodland want to be an encouragement to you by providing some amazing recipes that will hopefully make your day taste a little better. Not only do we want to help you, but you are helping us by purchasing this book. All of the proceeds will be donated to our Gateway Fund which was established for the purpose of investing in our facilities. These resources are being used as gateways to share the Good News of Jesus Christ. Enjoy the book and HAPPY EATING!

Dedication

Welcome to Woodland, the Community Church, a place that will show, teach and prepare you to share the love of Christ with others. This book is dedicated to those that will use the Gateway, our worship center. We hope this cookbook makes family and meal time even more enjoyable. Thank you to the contributors who gave us their favorite recipes to share with others.

Editor's Note

The most challenging part of compiling a cookbook is confirming that all recipes, ingredients and measurements are without error and come together to create something wonderful. We have read and proofed all of these recipes, but in case we missed something, or even missed an entire recipe, please understand the challenge of gathering, organizing, and printing over 300 recipes!

Contents

Staff Favorites 9

Appetizers and Beverages 23

Breads and Brunches 45

Vegetables and Side Dishes 63

Soups and Salads 83

Entrees 113

Desserts 163

Healthy Fare 225

Staff Favorites

"Then Jesus explained: "My nourishment comes from doing the will of God, who sent me, and from finishing his work."

John 4:34

Staff Favorites

The following recipes were submitted by our staff as some of their "favorites." These recipes are also listed under their appropriate categories, but we thought you would enjoy trying some of our staff members' favorite recipes.

Best-Ever Chocolate Fudge Layer Cake
Holly McAndrew, Administrative Assistant

1 pkg. (8 squares) Baker's semi-sweet baking chocolate, divided
1 pkg. chocolate cake mix (w/out pudding)
1 pkg. (4-serving size) Jell-o chocolate flavor instant pudding
4 eggs
1 cup Breakstone's or Knudsen sour cream
1/2 cup oil
1/2 cup water
1 tub (8 oz.) frozen Cool Whip topping
2 Tbsp. Planters sliced almonds

Preheat oven to 350. Grease 2 9" round baking pans. Chop 2 of the chocolate squares; set aside. Beat cake mix, dry pudding mix, eggs, sour cream, oil and water in large bowl with electric mixer on low speed just until moistened. Beat on medium speed 2 min. Stir in chopped chocolate. Spoon into prepared pans. Bake 30-35 min. or until wooden toothpick inserted in centers comes out clean. Cool in pans on wire racks 10 min. Loosen cakes from sides of pans. Invert onto racks; gently remove pans. Cool cakes completely. Place frozen whipped topping and remaining 6 chocolate squares in the microwaveable bowl. Microwave on HIGH for 1 1/2 min. or until chocolate is completely melted and mixture is smooth, stirring after 1 min. Let stand 15 min. to thicken. Place 1 cake layer on serving plate; top with 1/4 of the chocolate mixture and the second cake layer. Spread top and side with remaining chocolate mixture. Garnish with almonds. Store in refrigerator. Servings: 18

BBQ Green Beans
Andy Botts, Worship Arts Associate

1 lb. of green beans (cut, and drained)
1 can of tomato soup
1 large onion
6 slices of bacon (I prefer turkey bacon)
1/2 cup of brown sugar
1 cup of ketchup
1 can of French's crispy fried onions

Cut up the bacon and the onion into small pieces. Saute the onion and bacon, with butter in a medium skillet. Mix the tomato soup, ketchup, and brown sugar, then pour over bacon and onions. Pour entire mixture over green beans in a casserole dish. Bake at 350 for 25 minutes. Take out, put crispy onions on top, and put back in the oven for 5 more minutes, or until bubbling on top.

Broccoli Salad
Sylvia Kursawe, Administrative Assistant

1 head fresh broccoli, cut into bite size pieces
1/4 cup red onion, chopped
1/2 cup raisins
3 Tbsp. white wine vinegar
2 Tbsp. white sugar 1 cup mayonnaise
1 cup sunflower seeds

In a medium bowl, combine the broccoli, onion and raisins. In a small bowl, whisk together the vinegar, sugar and mayonnaise. Pour over broccoli mixture, and toss until well mixed. Refrigerate for at least two hours. Before serving, toss salad with crumbled bacon and sunflower seeds.

Bruleed Banana Splits
Dave Friss, Technical Director

2 Bananas
Vanilla Ice Cream
Cooking Torch
Granulated sugar
Caramel Sauce

Flip a baking sheet upside down on the counter, and cover with several sheets of heavy duty aluminum foil (create an airspace so you don't burn your counter). Quarter the unpeeled bananas. Fill the bottom of a bowl with the sugar, and press the cut side of the bananas into the sugar to coat. Place the sugared bananas on the foil cooking rig. Sprinkle with more sugar. Follow the manufacturer's instructions to ignite and operate the cooking torch. Apply the small blue triangle of flame nearest the tip of the torch to the first banana, using constant motion. The sugar should melt, then turn brown. Work the flame up and down the banana not leaving any sugar uncooked. Make sure to use constant motion so the fruit doesn't burn. Allow to cool for a few seconds, and then tapping lightly with a metal spoon to ensure that a crunch candy shell has been created. Repeat with the remaining bananas.

Drizzle a bit of caramel sauce on the bottom of the bowl in a zig zag pattern. Place four banana pieces in the bowl leaving a bit of space in the middle. Put a scoop of vanilla ice cream in the center of the bananas. Drizzle with more caramel sauce.

Makes two banana splits

Cha Cha's White Chicken Chili
Cindy Totty, Finance Director

1 Tbsp. vegetable oil	1 tsp. dried oregano
1 onion, chopped	1 tsp. ground cayenne pepper
3 cloves garlic, crushed	2 (14.5 oz.) cans chicken broth
1 (4 oz.) can jalapeno peppers	3 cups chopped chicken breast
1 (4 oz.) can chopped green chiles	3 (15 oz.) cans white beans
2 tsp. ground cumin	
1 cup shredded Monterey jack cheese	

Heat the oil in a large saucepan over medium-low heat. Slowly cook and stir the onion until tender. Mix in the garlic, jalapeno, green chile peppers, cumin, oregano and cayenne. Continue to cook and stir the mixture until tender, about 3 minutes. Mix in the chicken broth, chicken and white beans. Simmer 15 minutes, stirring occasionally. Remove the mixture from heat. Slowly stir in the cheese until melted. Serve warm.

Cheesy Chicken Spaghetti
Tina Yoder, Director of Ministry Involvement

1 cut up chicken	1 large jar cheese whiz
1 can cream of mushroom soup	1 can cream of celery soup
1 stick of butter	1 cup diced onion
1 cup of small diced bell pepper	
1 large package of thin spaghetti	

Boil chicken until tender. Drain broth into a pot and reserve to cook the spaghetti in. Cut up the chicken into bite-sized pieces and set aside. Cook the onion and bell pepper in the butter on the stove until the onions are clear and peppers tender. Break up the dry spaghetti, and then cook in the broth per package instruction while the onions are cooking. Add the cheese whiz and soups to the onions and simmer until warm and the cheese is melted and mixed well. Remove spaghetti, drain and put back in a large pot. Add the diced chicken and cheese/onion sauce to the spaghetti and mix well. Season to taste with salt and pepper. Turn into 2 buttered casserole dishes (one for you and one for a neighbor). Bake uncovered at 350 for 30-40 minutes.

Chicken Caesar Salad
Banks Corl, Associate Pastor of Strategic Growth

Rotisserie Chicken
1/2 cup Cardini's Original Caesar dressing, or similar
6 cups hand shredded romaine lettuce
2 cups garlic croutons
1/2 cup pre-shredded parmesan cheese

When you don't have much time, but you want to eat something that tastes great and is balanced (protein, veggies, some tasty carbs) so an hour later you don't feel hungry, or guilty, or crummy, where do you turn? Chicken Caesar, of course! Yes, I admit, there were those times in seminary I had 20 minutes and just grabbed a box of Cheese Nips and pretty much downed it for dinner and felt OK because I was in my mid-20's and my body could pretty much turn anything with caloric content into healthy bone, sinew, and muscle. But as Paul wrote, "When I became a man, I put away childish things..." So, forsaking my bachelor days motto, "If it takes longer to fix than eat, it, it's off the menu," and pressing on toward healthy, tasty, and quick here is my favorite Caesar Salad solution. I prefer the Cardini Original classic dressing, since that was the original Caesar dressing and honestly, tastes wonderful. It is a creamy dressing that has the garlic and spices already added to perfect proportions.

Wash, separate, and lay out the romaine on paper towels. Hand shred to a fairly fine consistency (fork ready) into a large mixing or salad bowl. I prefer hand shredding because it creates a better texture, and once you get the hang of it, it's nearly as fast as chopping and much better for taking out any left over frustration from your day. Then filet out both chicken breasts from the roasted chicken and remove the skin. You can find some additional white meat next to the wings underneath if you need more. Cut the chicken into bite sized pieces or longer strips. Mix in the dressing, cheese, and chicken. If serving right away, mix in the garlic croutons. If not, then add them at the last minute so they don't get soggy.

Clam Chowder
Tim Passmore, Pastor

2 large cans of clams
10 strips of bacon
8 small red potatoes
2 cups of whole milk
Salt and pepper

1 cup of clam juice
1 large sweet onion
2 cup of cream
4 Tbsp. of butter
Hot sauce

I don't cook. I don't heat up, reheat, assemble or microwave. I don't eat leftovers or anything that Jennifer must do the "smell check" on. If Jennifer isn't there to cook, I eat Reese Cups and Diet Coke and call it a meal. So, when asked to contribute to this cookbook, I really had nothing. Occasionally I'll use the toaster to make a PB&J (I like it on toasted bread), but other than that, I have no cooking experience. And then I remembered a rainy Saturday about 6 years ago when I was in between boats and looking for a new hobby. This was, of course "pre-medication." If you don't know what I am referring to then you need to read my book, **One Fry Short** *and catch up on my history. Jennifer loved to cook and so I thought we could make something together. I chose clam chowder because I was longing for a boat and the rainy weather was just right for soup. I have never made this soup or anything else since. Oh, the soup was great and Jennifer makes it for me often, but cooking was not to be my next new hobby.*

Cut up potatoes in to cubes. Cook the potatoes in the clam juice until fork tender. Cook the bacon and set aside. Chop the onions and sauté them in a large soup pot until they are golden brown. Add the cream, milk and the potatoes with the juice. Add the two cans of clams, salt, pepper and some hot sauce. Crumble the bacon in and allow to simmer for an hour.

Chicken Casserole
Lee Ann Martin, Marketing and Design Coordinator

3 cups chicken, cooked and cube
1/2 cup mayonnaise
1 cup cooked rice
1 sleeve Ritz crackers, crushed
1 can cr. of mushroom soup
4 tsp. lemon juice
1 small sour cream (8 oz.)
1 stick melted margarine

Mix everything except Ritz crackers and margarine. Place in 3-quart casserole. Top with mixture of margarine and cracker crumbs. Bake 45 minutes at 350. *Hint* - crush the crackers in a large zip lock bag. Easy to crush with your hands or a rolling pin!

Country Style Chicken Medley
Melanie Richards, Administrative Assistant

Vegetable Mixture:
1/4 cup sweet butter
1 can of whole kernel corn, drained
1 tsp. basil leaves
4 cups peeled, sliced potatoes
1 tsp. salt
1/4 tsp. nutmeg

Chicken and crumb mixture:
Enough graham cracker crumbs to coat chicken
1 tsp. salt
1/3 cup melted butter
1 1/2 tsp. basil leaves
3 pounds frying chicken, cut into pieces

Melt 1/4 cup butter in 13x9x2 inch baking dish. Add sliced potatoes and corn. Sprinkle with 1 tsp salt, 1 tsp basil, and 1/4 tsp nutmeg. Set aside. Combine graham cracker crumbs, 1 tsp salt and 1 tsp basil; mix well. Dip chicken into 1/3 cup melted butter, then into crumb mixture to coat; place skin side up on top of vegetable mixture. Sprinkle with 1/2 tsp basil. Cover tightly with foil; bake in center of 375 oven for 75 minutes or until tender. Remove foil; bake for 10 minutes longer to brown. Yields 4 to 6 servings.

Deep-Fried Pickles
Derek Berg, Communications and Technology Coordinator

Egg Wash:
2 cups milk   2 eggs
Pinch lemon pepper   Pinch dill weed
In a baking dish, whisk all ingredients together.

Breading:
2 1/2 cups cornmeal   1 1/2 cups all-purpose flour
1/2 cup lemon pepper   1/2 cup dill weed
4 tsp. paprika   2 tsp. garlic salt
Pinch cayenne pepper, or more to taste
Combine all ingredients in a baking dish.

In a deep fryer, heat oil to 375. Carefully add chilled pickle spears to the hot oil and fry for about 3 1/2 minutes or until golden. Remove to a paper towel-lined plate to drain. Serve with ranch dressing.

Fabulous Cheesecake
Keith Martin, Worship Arts Pastor

Filling:
3 (8 oz.) cream cheese   4 eggs
1 1/2 cup sugar
Crust :
52 vanilla wafers (crushed)   1 stick margarine
Topping:
8 oz. sour cream   1/2 cup sugar

Crust - Crush vanilla wafers, pour into spring form pan. Melt margarine and pour over wafers. Pat into bottom of pan.
Filling - mix all ingredients together well and pour over crust. Bake in 350 oven for 45 min.
Topping - mix sour cream and sugar together & pour over cake. Continue baking for 15 minutes longer.

Mexican Pizza
Mike Wilder, Children's Director

Crust:
2 boxes corn muffin mix
2 eggs
4 tsp. melted butter
1 1/2 cups milk
1 cup frozen corn kernels
Extra-virgin olive oil or vegetable oil, for drizzling

Topping
2 tablespoons extra-virgin or vegetable oil, 2 turns of the pan
1 pound ground beef
1 small onion, finely chopped
1 tsp. chili powder
2 tsp. ground cumin
2 tsp. cayenne sauce
Salt
2 1/2 cups shredded cheddar or jack cheese
1/2 red bell pepper, chopped
1 small can, 2 1/4 ounces sliced chiles or jalapenos, drained
2 scallions, chopped
2 small vine ripe tomatoes, seeded and diced
2 tsp. drained sliced green olives (salad olives)
1 to 2 tsp. chopped cilantro leaves, optional garnish
Mild to medium taco sauce to pass at table, about 1 cup

Preheat oven to 400. Mix together 2 packages muffin mix with 2 eggs, 4 tablespoons melted butter (melt in microwave 30 seconds), 1 1/2 cups milk and frozen corn kernels. Wipe a nonstick skillet with a little extra or vegetable oil and pour in the muffin mix. Use a large skillet, 10 to 12 inch. Choose a pan with oven safe handle or, double-wrap handle with foil to protect it in the oven. Place pan in oven and bake 12 to 15 minutes in center of the oven until light golden in color. Brown the meat over medium high heat in a second skillet in extra or vegetable oil, 2 turns of the pan. Add onions and spices and cook meat 5 minutes more. Remove cornbread from oven and top with meat, cheese, and veggies. Add pan back to oven and cook 5 minutes more to melt cheese. Garnish with cilantro, optional. Cut into 8 wedges and serve the deep dish pan pizza from the skillet. Pass taco sauce at the table to sprinkle on top.

Georgia Style Chocolate Cake
Carla Kelly, Administrative Assistant

2 cups flour
1/2 tsp. salt
1 stick butter
3/4 cup vegetable oil
1/2 cup buttermilk
2 eggs

2 cups sugar
1 cup water
3 Tbsp. cocoa
1 tsp. soda
1 tsp. vanilla

Frosting:
1 stick butter 1 (16 oz.) confectioners' sugar
1 Tbsp. cocoa
6 Tbsp. evaporated milk
2 tsp. vanilla
1 cup chopped pecans

Combine in 2 qt. pan, bring to simmer. DO NOT BOIL. Pour over cake when cool.

Cake:
Combine flour, sugar and salt in large bowl; set aside. Mix water, butter, cocoa and vegetable oil in 2 quart sauce pan. Bring to boil and add to flour mixture. Combine soda, buttermilk and vanilla. Put into flour mixture. Add eggs, beating well after each addition. Pour into 11"x16" cookie sheet with sides. Bake 20 min. Frost with above frosting.

Low-Fat Zucchini Fries
Coley Mays, Student Minister

Canola oil cooking spray   1/2 cup whole wheat flour
1/2 cup all-purpose flour   2 Tbsp. cornmeal
1 tsp. salt   1/2 tsp.-1 tsp. pepper
3 medium zucchinis, cut into 1/2-inch-by-3-inch sticks
2 egg whites, lightly beaten

Preheat oven to 475. Coat large baking sheet with cooking spray. Combine flours, cornmeal, salt, and pepper. Dip zucchini pieces in egg whites and coat with the flour mixtures. Place the zucchini on the baking sheet. Coat all exposed sides with cooking spray. Bake on the center rack for 7 minutes. Turn the zucchini and coat any floury spots with cooking spray. Continue to bake until golden and just tender, about 5 more minutes.

Shrimp and Tortellini in Cheese Sauce
Don Bailey, Counseling Director

1 lb. large shrimp   1 lb. three cheese tortellini
1 16 oz. jar of parmesan cheese sauce   1 roma tomato, diced
2 green onions, chopped   1 Tbsp. garlic
1/2 cup white wine   2 Tbsp. olive oil
1 tsp. Heart Healthy seasoning (Italian) Italian bread

Cook tortellini in salted water for 6-8 min. Drain and set aside. In large skillet, add olive oil and shrimp and cook until shrimp is pink (do not overcook). Add garlic, onions, tomatoes and seasoning. Simmer 2 minutes until onions are cooked. Add cheese sauce and white wine and simmer until hot. Serve with tossed salad with sun-dried tomato dressing and a green vegetable or corn-on-the-cob. Use Italian bread to dip up the excess sauce. YUMMY!!

Spinach Artichoke Dip
Jennifer Passmore, Preschool Director

1 package frozen chopped spinach
1 8 oz. package of cream cheese
1 cup mayo
1 cup grated mozzarella cheese
1 can artichoke hearts cut up
1 cup of parmesan cheese
Salt and pepper
1/2 tsp. garlic powder

Cook spinach in the microwave for 5 minutes, cool and press out all of the water. Mix all the ingredients and put in an oven safe casserole dish. Bake at 350 for 30 minutes. We eat this with nacho chips or French bread.

Sweet and Sour Meatballs
Laura Torrisi, Recreation Coordinator

1 ½ pounds ground beef	1 tsp. shortening
2/3 cup cracker crumbs	2 tsp. cornstarch
1/3 cup minced onion	1/2 cup brown sugar (packed)
1 egg	1/3 cup chopped green pepper
1 can (14 oz.) pineapple tidbits, drained (reserve syrup)	
1 ½ tsp. salt	1/3 cup vinegar
1/4 cup milk; for meatballs	1 Tbsp. soy sauce

Mix thoroughly beef, crumbs, onion, egg, salt, ginger and milk. Shape mixture by rounded tablespoonfuls into balls. Melt shortening in large skillet; brown and cook meatballs. Remove meatballs: keep warm Pour fat from skillet

Mix cornstarch and sugar. Stir in reserved pineapple syrup, vinegar, and soy sauce until smooth. Pour into skillet: cook over medium heat, stirring constantly, until mixture thickens and boils. Boil and stir 1 minute. Add meatballs, pineapple tidbits and green pepper heat through.

Taco Ring
Jill Atchley, School of Fine Arts Director

2 packages of crescent rolls
1 lb. ground beef
Small chopped onion
1 cup prepared salsa
1 cup shredded cheese
Garnish- lettuce, tomato, sour cream, etc.

Pizza pan or cookie sheet is ideal. Unroll the crescent rolls and layout like a clock-face layout at 12, 3, 6 & 9, then lay a second row overlapping the first. With the 2nd package of rolls, lay one crescent roll in between each roll from the first package. Press seams together at overlaps. Cook ground beef & onion, drain. Add salsa and cheese. Spoon ingredients into the area created by overlapping rolls. Roll the tips of the crescent rolls over the mixture & "tuck" under center. You should end up with a ring. Bake at the temperature & time listed on the crescent roll package.

Appetizers and Beverages

"I am the bread of life. No one who comes to me will ever be hungry again. Those who believe in me will never thirst."

John 6:35

Appetizers and Beverages

Bang Bang Shrimp
Pam Herrington

1/2 cup mayonnaise
1/4 cup Thai sweet chili sauce
Few drops of hot chili sauce
1 lb. shelled and deveined shrimp
Corn starch
Cooking oil
Lettuce, several scallions, chopped

Mix mayo and chili sauces - set aside roll/coat shrimp with cornstarch. Fry shrimp in deep fat until golden brown. Drain shrimp on paper towel Put shrimp in bowl - add chili sauce and mix together. Serve in lettuce line bowl with chopped scallions.

"Baptist" Champagne
Andreah Wellman

1 2 liter bottle (67 oz.), ginger ale
2 48 oz. bottles (96 oz.), white grape juice
** Decorative Ice Ring

Chill grape juice and ginger ale. Pour into punch bowl over decorative ice ring. ** To make decorative ice ring, freeze some of the same ingredients in a Bundt pan, filled about 1/3 full. (Don't use water for ice ring- it dilutes the punch too much as it thaws). I put maraschino cherries in the bottom and mint leaves to add color. You can use any fruit you wish. Serves 20. This punch is great with all types of reception foods. This is an easy punch to make. Always a hit at our church activities, or when family and friend get together.

Bean Salsa
Megan Johnson

1 can black beans (rinsed/drained)
1 can corn
1 chopped red pepper (any color will do)
1/2 large onion chopped (red or Vidalia)
1/4 cup chopped cilantro
1 tomato diced (grape tomatoes are great for this)
1/2 cup light Italian dressing (can use regular)
1/2 tsp. Tabasco/hot sauce
1/2 tsp. garlic powder
1 Tbsp. lime juice (may substitute w/lemon)

Mix all ingredients. Let marinate over night if possible. *Can be used as a condiment with meat as well.

Black Eyed Pea Salsa/ Southern Caviar
Shea Haupt

2 cans black-eyed peas, drained
1 can black beans, drained and rinsed
2 cups whole kernel corn (canned or frozen)
1 bunch green onions, chopped
2 cans Rotel tomatoes
1 clove crushed garlic
1 Tbsp. sugar
1/2 cup red wine vinegar
1 red and 1 yellow bell pepper, chopped

Combine all in a large bowl. Refrigerate several hours to over night before serving. Serve as a dip with tortilla chips or as a salad.

Blue Cheese Dip
Jannon Pierce

16 oz. sour cream
4 oz. blue cheese or gorgonzola, crumbled
2-3 splashes of Worcestershire
2-3 splashes of red wine vinegar
Salt
Pepper
Heaping Tbsp. of chopped garlic in jar

Mix all ingredients and chill for 2-3 hours before serving with veggies or Scoops Frito Chips.

"Boo's" Orange Julius
Andreah Wellman

6 oz. frozen orange juice, don't thaw
1 cup water
1/2 cup sugar

1 cup milk
12 small ice cubes
1 tsp. vanilla

Place all in a blender. Blend well and serve. This is so refreshing, and a nice treat to serve guests in Florida!

Buffalo Chips
Pam Herrington

1 lb. hot (spicy) pork sausage
1 lb. Velveeta Cheese
1/2 tsp. garlic salt
3 loaves cocktail rye

1 lb. ground beef
1/4 tsp. ground red pepper
1 tsp. oregano or marjoram

Brown and drain sausage & ground beef. Cheese, cubed and melted in with above after meat is drained. Add red pepper, garlic salt & oregano after cheese is melted. Spread on cocktail rye. Refrigerate until set. Bake at 400 for 5 minutes. Use petite rye (3 loaves) makes 80 or more. Can be frozen on cookie sheets before baking and then just bake as many as you want as you want at a time.

Buffalo Chicken Dip
Katrina West

4 boneless, skinless chicken breasts
1 (12oz.) bottle Frank's hot sauce
2 (8 oz.) packages cream cheese
1 (16 oz.) ranch salad dressing
8 oz. shredded sharp cheddar, Monterey jack or combination

In large saucepan, boil the chicken in water until cooked through (about 15 minutes), drain and shred. Preheat oven to 350. In a 13x9 inch baking pan, combine the shredded chicken with the hot sauce, spreading to form an even layer.

In a large saucepan over medium heat, combine the cream cheese and ranch dressing, stirring until smooth and hot. Pour the mixture evenly over the chicken. Bake uncovered for 20 minutes, then sprinkle the shredded cheese over the top and bake uncovered for another 10 minutes. Let stand 10 minutes before serving.

Caramel Pop Corn
Louise Riley

1 bag of popped popcorn
1/4 to 1/2 cup butter or margarine
1/2 cup brown sugar, packed
8 large marshmallows (or 1 cup of mini marshmallows)

Pop the bag of microwave popcorn, and while it is popping melt the butter in a saucepan and stir, add marshmallows and brown sugar and melt. Make sure you stir it and let it bubble a bit, then just pour over the popcorn in another bowl. Mix well. It is best eaten right away, and be ready to eat the whole thing!!

Clam Dip
Tryla Falbo

8 oz. of cream cheese
½ cup mayo
Garlic (about a Tbsp. or to taste)
1 can minced clams
4 Tbsp. of reserved clam juice
Little lemon juice
Pinch of salt
1/2 tsp. Worcestershire

Beat all ingredients together. Let set over night so flavors can meld. Serve with potato chips.

Crab Cheese Dip
Tryla Falbo

1 can of crab
1 Tbsp. onion
¼ cup milk
8 oz. cream cheese
½ cup mayo
Dash of Worcestershire or Tabasco

Beat all ingredients together and let set over night. Heat in 350 degree oven, covered. Eat warm with crackers.

Cheese Dip
Jennifer Passmore

8 oz. of sour cream
8 oz. cream cheese
2-4 ½ oz. cans of green chili
8 oz. package of ham
16 oz. sharp cheddar cheese
4 green onions chopped
1 tsp. of Worcestershire sauce
Large bread round loaf

Mix all ingredients. Cut top off of bread and scoop out bread. Fill bread bowl with the cheese mixture and bake at 350 for 1 hour. Serve with corn chips or French bread cubed.

Cheese Ball
Samantha Slade

2- 8 oz. pkgs. cream cheese, at room temp
1 small can crushed pineapple
1/4 cup chopped green pepper
2 Tbsp. chopped onion
1 Tbsp. seasoning salt
1/2 cup chopped pecans
1 1/2 cups chopped pecans to cover

Combine all ingredients except 1 1/2 cups chopped pecans. Form into 1 large or 2 small cheese balls. Roll in 1 1/2 cups chopped pecans until outside is covered. Serve with crackers.

Deep-Fried Pickles
Derek Berg

Egg Wash:
2 cups milk   2 eggs
Pinch lemon pepper   Pinch dill weed
In a baking dish, whisk all ingredients together.

Breading:
2 1/2 cups cornmeal   1 1/2 cups all-purpose flour
1/2 cup lemon pepper   1/2 cup dill weed
4 tsp. paprika   2 tsp. garlic salt
Pinch cayenne pepper, or more to taste
Combine all ingredients in a baking dish.

In a deep fryer, heat oil to 375 degrees. Carefully add chilled pickle spears to the hot oil and fry for about 3 1/2 minutes or until golden. Remove to a paper towel-lined plate to drain. Serve with ranch dressing.

Dilly Dip
Marcia Timmins

2/3 cup mayonnaise
1 cup sour cream
1 tsp. dill weed
1 tsp. onion juice or grated onion
1 tsp. chopped parsley
1 tsp. horseradish
1 tsp. seasoned salt
Dash of red pepper or Tabasco sauce

Mix and refrigerate several hours before serving. Makes a great veggie dip.

Festive Olive Ball
Linda Jesel

2 cup finely grated Sharp Cheddar Cheese
1/2 cup (1 stick) soft butter
1 cup sifted flour
2 Tbsp. Tabasco Sauce
36-48 stuffed green olives

Beat butter and cheese together. Blend in remaining ingredients except olives. Drain and dry olives before rolling dough around them. Cover olives with dough, and roll into a ball. Bake at 350-400 degree oven for 15 minutes. Interesting flavor!

Hidden Valley Ranch Dip
Pam Herrington

1 oz. packet of original ranch party dip
1 pint sour cream
1/4 cup bacon bits
1 cup shredded cheddar cheese
chips, crackers, vegetables

Mix first 4 ingredients. Serve with chips, crackers or vegetables.

Inside-out English Muffin Grilled Cheese
Diana Burnside

4 sandwich-size English muffins
Butter, softened
8 slices sharp white cheddar cheese (or colby cheese)
4 1/8 in. thick slices beefsteak tomato
salt and pepper, to taste

Heat a cast-iron skillet or griddle over medium to low heat. Lightly spread the inside of each English muffin half with butter. Arrange the muffins buttered sides out and build 4 sandwiches using a slice of cheese, tomato slice, some salt and pepper and another cheese slice. Place in pan and cook, turning once or twice, until the cheese is melted and the muffins are golden brown, about 8 minutes. Serves 4.

Kay's Fresh Salsa
Lee Ann Martin

2 cans regular stewed tomatoes
1 medium onion, chopped
2-3 fresh, seeded, chopped small jalapeno peppers
2 garlic cloves, chopped
Small bunch cilantro leaves, some stems, chopped
2 fresh tomatoes, diced
Juice of one lime
Salt and pepper, to taste

Place stewed tomatoes in blender. Pulse, being careful not to puree, but keep in small pieces. Stir in remaining ingredients. Let stand for 1 hour.

Layered Nacho Dip
Shea Haupt

1 16 oz. can refried beans
1 6 oz. carton avocado dip
4 1/2 can chopped black olives
1 sm. onion finely chopped
1/2 pkg. taco seasoning
8 oz. sour cream
2 lrg. tomatoes, diced
4 oz. can chopped green chilies 1 1/2 cup shredded Monterey Jack cheese

Combine beans and seasoning mix. Spread bean mixture evenly in a 12x8 dish. Layer remaining ingredients in order listed. Serve with corn chips or tortilla chips!

Lemon and Mint Iced Tea
Becky Wessel

8 cups water divided
4 family sized tea bags (orange pekoe or Pekoe cut black tea)
2 sprigs fresh mint
3/4 cup white sugar
1/4 cup lemon juice

Bring 4 cups water to a boil in medium sauce pan. Remove from heat. Add tea bags and mint to pan. Steep for 20 minutes. Discard tea bags and mint. Combine sugar and lemon juice in a glass measuring cup. Add 1/2 cup hot tea mixture. Stir until sugar dissolves. Pour sugar mixture into rest of tea in pan. Pour into 2 quart pitcher and add 4 cups cold water. Stir. Serve over ice.

Marinated Crackers
Samantha Slade

1 large bag oyster crackers
1 pkg. Hidden Valley Original Ranch Mix
1/4 to 1/3 cup of oil

Toss all ingredients together and pour into large sheet pan. Bake at 300 for 20 minutes. Cool. Put in an airtight container.

Mississippi Sin
Charlotte Vaughn

1/2 cup sour cream
1/3 cup mild green chili peppers, chopped
2 cups cheddar cheese, grated
1 dash Worcestershire sauce
8 oz. cream cheese
1 loaf French bread
1/3 cup green onion, chopped
1 bag Frito Scoop chips
½ cup chopped sandwich ham
3 dashes of Tabasco sauce

Mix first eight ingredients. Cut top of French bread and hollow out inside. Fill with mixture. Bake for one hour at 350 degrees, wrapped in foil. Serve with extra bread and Frito Scoop chips.

Momma's Spicy Shrimp Appetizer
Andreah Wellman

3 pounds med - large shrimp
2 packages of Good Seasons Zesty Italian Salad Dressing mix
4 lemons
1 3 oz. package Zatarain's Crab Boil Seasoning
1 Tbsp. salt

Cook shrimp in 3 quart water with the crab boil seasoning, and 1 lemon rind. When pink, drain. Squeeze 3 lemons over cooked shrimp, and mix 1 package Good Seasons as directed on package. Add the other package of dressing, dry. Combine all, and chill overnight. Serve with crackers, and enjoy.

Monster Dip
Tom, Debi, and Kathy Jo Cole

1 small regular Velveeta cheese
1 small Mexican Velveeta cheese
16 oz. can refried beans
1 can Rotel diced tomatoes and green chilies
16oz. Pace Picante sauce
1 bag nacho chips jalapeno peppers (optional)

Cut both Velveeta cheese into small squares. Mix all ingredients in a crock pot on low heat. Stir as it heats until the cheese melts. Put nachos on plates dip the monster dip over them and enjoy

Pineapple Cheese Ball
Sandy Taylor

2 8 oz. packages cream cheese, softened
2 Tbsp. chopped green pepper, finely
2 Tbsp. chopped onion, finely
1/3 cup crushed pineapple, drained
2 tsp. seasoned salt
2 cups chopped pecans, divided

Beat cream cheese until smooth; add green pepper, onion, pineapple, seasoned salt, and 1 cup pecans, mixing well. Shape into ball and chill. Roll in remaining nuts and serve with crackers.

Pizza Dip
Reba Pearson

1 8 oz. pkg. cream cheese	1 jar of spaghetti sauce
1 pkg. of pepperoni	1 pkg. Italian shredded cheese

Layer: 1-cream cheese. 2-Spaghetti sauce. 3-Pepperoni. 4-Italian cheese. Bake at 400 degrees for 14 minutes, do not over cook. Serve with your favorite tortilla chips, I like the Scoops. This recipe actually comes from my sister-in-law, April Pearson. GREAT FOR THOSE GATOR FOOTBALL GAMES : -)

Pizza Bangers
The Brian Hall Family

Pizza Dough from Publix in the Deli/any flavor (or you can use frozen bread dough)
Pepperoni (we use turkey)
Garlic powder
Pizza sauce for dipping

Heat oven to 350. Separate dough into small balls (snack size) put one pepperoni inside each, make sure it is not showing. Grease cookie sheet or we use our pizza stone with corn meal. You can "butter" the tops and sprinkle garlic powder or you can just roll the balls in some garlic powder. Put them on the sheet or stone and cook for 15-18 min. until golden brown. Serve with your favorite pizza sauce for dipping. ENJOY! Great after school snack! 1 frozen bread loaf makes 12-15 bangers. 1 deli fresh pizza dough makes 12-15 bangers.

Puppy Chow Snack
Linda Rehder

1 (12 oz.) bag chocolate chips
1/2 cup butter/margarine (1 stick)
1 (large box) 3 cup powdered sugar
3/4 cup peanut butter
9 cup rice Chex cereal,

Melt chocolate chips, peanut butter together in microwave on high power for 1-1 1/2 minutes. Stir after 1 minute. Pour mixture over Rice Chex and mix until coated. Put powdered sugar in large paper bag (or very large Tupperware with lid) and add cereal mix. Shake until coated. Place on cookie sheets to dry. Enjoy this simple and yummy snack.

Raspberry Punch
Durst Family

2 liters of ginger ale
3/4 cup of powdered lemonade
16 oz. of frozen raspberries
4 cups of ice

In large punch bowl mix ginger ale and lemonade mix. Before serving, stir in raspberries and ice. (Do not add any water.) Plain yellow lemonade powder mix turns pink because of the berries. Even 'store brand' ginger ale tastes great and is inexpensive. A great party drink!

Sausage Balls
Samantha Slade

1 lb. hot sausage
8 oz. fine shredded cheddar cheese
2 1/3 cup Bisquick mix
Dash cayenne pepper

Combine sausage and cheese together in a large bowl. Add Bisquick and cayenne pepper and blend thoroughly. Roll into 1 in. balls and place on an ungreased baking sheet. Bake at 350 degrees for 15 minutes.

Sausage Dip
Lynn Francisco

1 pkg. Jimmy Dean sage sausage
1 8 oz. cream cheese (softened)
1 can diced Rotel Tomatoes with Chiles

Cook sausage and drain. Put back in skillet or crock pot, add cream cheese and can of tomatoes. Mix well and serve with Scoops. Very easy and good.

Savory Chicken Crescent Squares
Durst Family

3 oz. cream cheese
2 Tbsp. melted butter (smooth together)
2 cups chopped chicken or turkey
1/4 tsp. salt
1/8 tsp. pepper
2 Tbsp. milk
1 Tbsp. chopped onion (mix together with cream cheese mixture)
1 can crescent rolls makes either
4 regular or 8 small potato chips

Put 1/2 cup of chicken mixture in the middle of each crescent square. Seal the corners to make a square. Brush the top with melted butter. Dip squares in crushed potato chips. Bake on ungreased cookie sheet at 350 degrees for 25 minutes.

Salsa
Sue Powell

2 large tomatoes or 5 Romas or 2 cups cherry tomatoes
6 sun-dried tomatoes
2 shallots or 1/4 sweet onion
1/4 red pepper 1 clove garlic
1 tsp. -1 Tbsp. jalapeno or to taste
Juice of 1 lemon
2 tsp. apple cider vinegar
1/2 tsp. sea salt
1-2 tsp. honey (I use agave sweetener)
1/2 cup cilantro, chopped

Prep: Presoak sun-dried tomatoes for at least 1 hour. Chop vegetables in food processor, drain juice and reserve. Place chopped vegetables in bowl and juice in blender. Add garlic, jalapeno, lemon juice, vinegar, sea salt and honey to juices in blender. Process until smooth. Mix into chopped vegetables with chopped cilantro. Allow to set for at least one hour for flavors to blend.

Scottish Eggs
Pam Herrington

9 hard boiled eggs peeled
1 pkg. sausage patties (18 patties)
Shake-n-Bake or breadcrumbs

Wrap 2 sausage patties around 1 egg (Form like a snowball). Roll in Shake-n-Bake (breadcrumbs). Bake for 45 minutes at 350 degrees on broiler pan so grease will drain away. Cut each egg into 4 wedges. Serve at room temperature.

7 Layer Taco Dip
Mindy Cress

1 can refried beans
1 cup sour cream
1 cup guacamole
1 tomato, chopped
1/2 cup chopped onion
2 cups cheddar cheese, shredded
1/2 cup black olives, chopped

Using a 9x9 glass bowl or pan, start layering ingredients; starting with refried beans, smoothing each out before adding the next ingredient. Serve cold with tortilla chips.

Shrimp Dip
Pam Herrington

2 lg cream cheese
1 pkg. Italian dressing
1 pkg. salad shrimp – thawed

1 can cream of shrimp soup
Squirt of lemon

Mix all together well.

Seven Layer Taco Dip
Heather Boswell

1 pkg. taco seasoning mix
1 8 oz. pkg. cream cheese, softened
2 cups shredded cheddar cheese
1 bunch green onions, chopped
1 small head lettuce, shredded
1 6 oz. can sliced black olives, drained
1 16 oz. can refried beans
1 16 oz. container sour cream
1 large tomato, chopped
1 green pepper, chopped
1 16 oz. jar salsa

In a medium bowl, blend the taco seasoning mix and refried beans. Spread the mixture onto a large serving platter. Mix the sour cream and cream cheese in a medium bowl. Spread over the refried beans. Top the layers with salsa. Place a layer of tomato, green pepper, green onions, and lettuce over the salsa and top with cheddar cheese. Garnish with black olives.

Slow Cooker Hot Crab Dip
Judy Daniels

1 package (8 oz.) cream cheese, softened
1/4 cup grated parmesan cheese
4 med. green onions, thinly sliced
1/4 cup mayonnaise
2 tsp. sugar
1 tsp. ground mustard
1 clove garlic, finely chopped
1 can (6 oz.) crabmeat, drained, cartilage removed and flaked
1/3 cup sliced almonds, toasted
Assorted crackers

Spray inside of 1-2 1/2 quart slow cooker with cooking spray. Mix all ingredients except crabmeat, almonds and crackers in a small bowl until well blended. Stir in crabmeat. Spoon into slow cooker. Cover and cook on low heat setting 1 hour 15 min. or until cheese is melted. Sprinkle with almonds. Serve warm with crackers. Dip will hold up to 3 hours. Makes 20 servings (2 Tbsp. each)

Spiced Nuts
Jannon Pierce

2 Tbsp. butter
1/4 cup brown sugar
2 Tbsp. water
1/4 tsp. ground cumin
1/4 tsp. cayenne pepper
1/4 tsp. cinnamon
1/2 tsp. salt and 2 cups mixed nuts

Mix spices and reserve. Heat nuts in a dry skillet and cook, stirring frequently until nuts begin to toast about 4 minutes. Transfer to a small bowl and set aside. Add butter, sugar, water and spices to the hot skillet and cook stirring until glaze forms, about 4 minutes. Return the nuts to the skillet and toss to coat with glaze. Cook for about 1-2 minutes or until the nuts are glazed and golden brown. Remove from the heat and transfer to a baking sheet lined with aluminum foil, separating with a fork. Let rest until cooked and the sugar has hardened, about 10 minutes.

Spinach Artichoke Dip
Jennifer Passmore

1 package frozen chopped spinach
1 8 oz. package of cream cheese
1 cup mayonnaise
1 cup grated mozzarella cheese
1 can artichoke hearts cut up
1 cup of parmesan cheese
Salt and pepper
1/2 teaspoon garlic powder

Cook spinach in the microwave for 5 minutes, cool and press out all of the water. Mix all the ingredients and put in an oven safe casserole dish. Bake at 350 for 30 minutes. We eat this with nacho chips or French bread.

Steve's Cheese Ball
Steve Wellman

1 8 oz. package Philadelphia cream cheese
1 Small jar of Kraft Old English Cheese
1 -Kraft Crumbled Blue Cheese
Garlic salt, pecans, olives

From room temperature, combine cream cheese, Old English Cheese and 1/2 of the package of blue cheese in a bowl. Add the garlic salt to your taste preference and place in the refrigerator until it becomes firm. Put the mixture on a plate and form by hand into a ball. Chop the pecans and press them on the ball to cover it completely. Garnish the cheese ball with parsley and olives.

Stuffed Mushroom Caps or Tomatoes
Tryla Falbo

8 large mushroom caps or tomatoes
1 oz. prosciutto, finely chopped
2 Tbsp. soft bread crumbs
2 Tbsp. of parsley
4 Tbsp. olive oil
1 clove of garlic
1 oz. of parmesan

Preheat oven to 375 degrees. Heat oil in pan. Add garlic, prosciutto & mushroom stocks. Cook 5 minutes. Mix with breadcrumbs, parmesan & parsley. Brush baking dish with olive oil and place stuffed mushrooms or tomatoes in glass baking dish. Then drizzle with olive oil over the tops. Bake uncovered about 20 minutes or so. Check after 20 and you decide.

Yellow Citrus Punch
Marge Wise

46 oz. pineapple juice
1/2 cup lemon juice
1 qt orange or pineapple sherbet

3 cups orange juice
2 quart ginger ale

Mix together. Makes 4 1/2 quarts / 24 - 6 oz. servings

Breads and Brunches

"Then Jesus took the loaves, gave thanks to God, and passed them out to the people."

John 6:11

Breads and Brunches

Amish Friendship Bread
Tina Yoder

1 (.25 oz.) package active dry yeast
1/4 cup warm water (110 degrees F/45 degrees C)
3 cups all-purpose flour, divided
3 cups white sugar, divided
3 cups milk, divided

Do not use metal containers or utensils. In a small bowl, dissolve yeast in water. Let stand 10 minutes. In a 2 quart container glass, plastic or ceramic container, combine 1 cup flour and 1 cup sugar. Mix thoroughly or flour will lump when milk is added. Slowly stir in 1 cup milk and dissolved yeast mixture. Cover loosely and let stand until bubbly. Consider this day 1 of the 10 day cycle. Leave loosely covered at room temperature. On days 2 thru 4; stir starter with a spoon. Day 5; stir in 1 cup flour, 1 cup sugar and 1 cup milk. Days 6 thru 9-stir only. Day 10-stir in 1 cup flour, 1 cup sugar and 1 cup milk. Remove 1 cup to make your first bread, give 2 cups to friends along with this recipe, and your favorite Amish Bread recipe. Store the remaining 1 cup starter in a container in the refrigerator, or begin the 10 day process over again (beginning with step 2). FOOTNOTES: Once you have made the starter, you will consider it Day One, and so ignore step 1 in this recipe and proceed with step 2. You can also freeze this starter in 1 cup measures for later use. Frozen starter will take at least 3 hours at room temperature to thaw before using.

Preheat oven to 350 degrees F (175 degrees C). Grease 2 (9x5 inch) loaf pans. In a large bowl, combine the Amish bread starter with oil, eggs, 2 cups flour, 1 cup sugar, 1 teaspoon ground cinnamon, 1/2 teaspoon salt, 1/2 teaspoon baking soda, 1 1/4 teaspoons baking powder, and 1 teaspoon vanilla. Mix well. Pour into prepared loaf pans. Bake in preheated oven for 50 to 60 minutes.

Angel Biscuits
Janice Sprowles

5 cups all purpose flour	1 cup shortening
1 tsp. baking soda	1 tsp. salt
3 tsp. baking powder	1/4 cup sugar
1 pkg. dry yeast	1/4 cup warm water
2 cups buttermilk	

Sift dry ingredients together. Cut in shortening. Dissolve yeast in warm water and combine with buttermilk. Add this to dry ingredients. Mix until all flour is moistened. Cover bowl and put in refrigerator overnight. When ready to use take out as much as needed, roll on floured board to 1/2 inch thick and cut out. Place in greased shallow pan and cover to rise - about 45 minutes to an hour. Bake at 400 degrees for 12 to 15 minutes until golden brown. Dough will keep several weeks in refrigerator. Makes about 6 dozen.

Apple Cinnamon French Toast
Megan Johnson

1 8oz. loaf of French bread	6 eggs
1 1/2 cups of milk	8 Tbsp. sugar, divided
1 tsp. vanilla	1/8 tsp. salt
1 1/2 tsp. cinnamon	4 Granny Smith apples
2 Tbsp. butter or margarine	vegetable oil spray
Maple syrup	

Spray 9 x13 baking dish with vegetable oil. Cut bread into 1-inch slices. Arrange closely in single layer in baking dish. In a bowl, beat eggs, whisk in milk, 3 tablespoons of sugar, vanilla and salt. Pour over bread. Combine remaining sugar with cinnamon. Peel, core, and slice apples. Cut into rings by slicing down one side of each apple. Place half of apples over bread. Sprinkle half of the sugar-cinnamon mixture evenly over the apples. Repeat layers. Cover and refrigerate 1 hour or over night. Preheat oven to 400 F. Cut butter into small pieces and arrange over apples. Bake uncovered, 30-35 minutes or until apples are tender. Let stand 5 minutes. Serve with syrup.

Breakfast Bacon and Egg Casserole
Carol Williams

5 slices buttered bread
4 eggs, slightly beaten
3/4 lb. grated sharp cheddar cheese
2 cup milk
1/2 lb. raw coarsely chopped bacon
1 tsp. dry mustard
1/2 tsp. salt

Trim crusts from bread and cube. In a greased 9x13 inch (or larger) baking pan, layer bread cubes, cheese and bacon. Mix eggs, milk, salt and mustard together and pour over layered ingredients.

Refrigerate overnight. Bake 1 hour at 350.

Bacon Swiss Bread
Marilyn Downer

1 loaf French bread (20")
2/3 cup butter, softened
1/3 cup chopped green onion
4 tsp. prepared mustard
5 slices processed Swiss cheese
5 bacon strips

Cut bread into 1" thick slices, leaving slices attached at bottom. In bowl, combine butter, onions and mustard. Spread on both sides of each slice of bread. Cut each cheese slice diagonally into 4 triangles; place between the slices of bread. Cut bacon in half width wise and then lengthwise; drape a piece over each slice. Place the loaf on a double thickness of heavy-duty foil. Bake at 400 degrees for 20 to 25 minutes or until bacon is crisp. Yield: 10 servings

Banana Butterscotch Bread
Linda Rehder

1 cup white sugar
1/2 cup margarine (1 stick)
1 tsp. salt
2 eggs
1 cup mashed ripe bananas (about 3 large)
1 tsp. vanilla
1 tsp. soda
3/4 cup butterscotch chips
1/4 cup brown sugar
3 Tbsp. soured milk (add 1 tsp. vinegar to milk to sour)
1 cup chopped walnuts or pecans (optional)

Mix together: white sugar, margarine, salt, vanilla, mashed bananas and eggs. Mix together: soured milk and baking soda before adding to batter. Fold in nuts if desired. Pour into large bread pan. Sprinkle with brown sugar and then with butterscotch chips. Bake 350 degrees about 1 hour or until toothpick comes out clean from center of bread.

Best Ever Short Bread
Mindy Cress

1 cup butter
1 cup sugar
1 large egg
1 tsp. vanilla
2 tsp. baking powder
3 cups flour

Preheat oven to 350 degrees. Cream butter and sugar. Add egg and vanilla and blend well. Add baking powder and flour. Mix until blended. Can either be rolled out or spooned onto an ungreased sheet pan. Bake approximately 6 to 7 minutes. Makes 2 dozen. *Note: Dough can be tinted with food coloring, shaped into rolls, cut with cookie cutters or even stuffed with jam. For chocolate dough add 3 oz melted chocolate.

Breakfast Pizza
Steve Wellman

1 package refrigerated crescent rolls
3 eggs
1 cup cheddar cheese, shredded
12 oz. sausage or turkey sausage, cooked and drained
1/4 cup milk
1 cup frozen southern style hash browns, thawed
1/4 cup finely chopped onions
1/4 cup finely chopped green peppers
1/4 teaspoon garlic salt
Salt and pepper, to taste

Preheat oven to 375 degrees. Press dough against bottom and sides of greased 12"pizza pan, pinch seams together to form a crust. Top with sausage and hash browns. In a small bowl, beat eggs with milk and add seasonings. Pour over pizza crust. Sprinkle the top with cheese. Bake for 20-30 minutes or until golden brown. Cut into wedges with pizza cutter and serve warm. Serves 8, (or 4 if bigger slices.)

Crab Quiche
Sharon Willis

4 oz. mushrooms
3 eggs slightly beaten
1 cup sour cream
1/2 tsp. Worcestershire sauce
3/4 tsp. salt
1 cup grated Swiss cheese
3 oz. can onion rings
1 9 in. pie shell
1 pkg. frozen imitation crab meat, thawed

Mix all ingredients together. Bake at 300, 55-60 minutes. EASY.

Chocolate Chip Pumpkin Bread
Shea Haupt

3 cups white sugar
1 (15 oz.) canned pumpkin
1 cup vegetable oil
2/3 cup water
4 eggs
3 1/2 cups of flour
1 tsp. ground cinnamon
1 tsp. ground nutmeg
2 tsp. baking soda
1 1/2 tsp. salt
1 cup mini semi-sweet chocolate chips
1/2 chopped walnuts or pecans

Preheat oven to 350. Grease and flour 3 9x5 loaf pans. In a large bowl combine sugar and next 4 ingredients. Beat until smooth. Blend in flour and next 4 ingredients. Fold in chocolate chips and nuts. Fill pans to 1/2-3/4 full. Bake for 1 hour or more, until inserted knife comes out clean. Cool on racks before removing from pans. Can also use muffin pans, just reduce cooking time.

Doris' Coffeecake
Marge Wise

2 cups flour
1/2 tsp. salt
1 tsp. baking powder
1/2 cup brown sugar
1 cup buttermilk

1/2 tsp. cinnamon
1 tsp. soda
1 cup sugar
2/3 cup butter
2 eggs

Mix all the dry ingredients together. Cut in butter. Mix the buttermilk and eggs. Add dry ingredients and mix slightly. Let stand in refrigerator overnight. In the morning, put in a greased 9x13 pan. Sprinkle top with 1/2 tsp cinnamon, 1/2 cup brown sugar, 1/4 - 1/2 tsp nutmeg, and 1/3 cup or more of chopped nuts. Bake at 350 degrees until golden brown.

Cinnamon Rolls
Tina & Sydney Yoder

3/4 cup milk
3 1/4 cups all-purpose flour
1/4 cup white sugar
1/4 cup water
1 cup brown sugar, packed
1/2 cup margarine, softened

1/4 cup margarine, softened
1 (.25 oz.) package instant yeast
1/2 teaspoon salt
1 egg
1 tsp. ground cinnamon
1/2 cup raisins (optional)

Frosting
3 cups confectioners' sugar
1 1/2 tsp. vanilla extract

1/3 cup butter, softened
1 1/2 tsp. milk

Heat the milk in a small saucepan until it bubbles, then remove from heat. Mix in margarine; stir until melted. Let cool until lukewarm. In a large mixing bowl, combine 2 1/4 cup flour, yeast, sugar and salt; mix well. Add water, egg and the milk mixture; beat well. Add the remaining flour, 1/2 cup at a time, stirring well after each addition. When the dough has just pulled together, turn it out onto a lightly floured surface and knead until smooth, about 5 minutes. Cover the dough with a damp cloth and let rest for 10 minutes. Meanwhile, in a small bowl, mix together brown sugar, cinnamon, softened margarine. Roll out dough into a 12x9 inch rectangle. Spread dough with margarine/sugar mixture. Sprinkle with raisins if desired. Roll up dough and pinch seam to seal. Cut into 12 equal size rolls and place cut side up in 12 lightly greased muffin cups. Cover and let rise until doubled, about 30 minutes. Preheat oven to 375 degrees (190 degrees C). Bake in the preheated oven for 20 minutes, or until browned. Remove from muffin cups to cool. Serve warm frosting In a medium bowl, stir together confectioners' sugar, 1/3 cup butter, vanilla and milk. Let rolls cool slightly then spread with frosting.

Cranberry Yogurt Muffins
Larry Wise

1 cup rolled oats
1/2 cup vegetable oil
1 cup yogurt
(I used 6 oz. cherry vanilla yogurt and 2 oz. of sour cream)
1/2 cup brown sugar
1 egg
1 cup flour
1/2 tsp. salt
1/2 tsp. soda
1 tsp. baking powder
3/4 cup nuts (I used walnuts)
1 can cranberries (I used a half bottle maraschino cherries, Drained.)

Soak oats in yogurt for several minutes. Add oil, sugar and egg; beat well. Sift together dry ingredients. Before stirring, sprinkle the cranberries, (chopped in half) over flour mixture. Bake at 400 degrees for 20 minutes. Makes 12 regular muffins or 6 extra large size muffins.

Egg Brunch Quiche
Wendy Pittman

1 1/2 cups cheddar cheese, shredded
1 1/2 cups mozzarella cheese, shredded
1/2 cup green onions, chopped
1/2 red pepper, chopped
8 oz. ham, cut in julienne strips or small pieces
1/2 cup flour
1 3/4 cup milk
2 Tbsp. parsley
8 eggs, beaten

Cook onions and peppers until tender. In greased, 13x9 in. pan put half the cheese. Spread onions and peppers on top, then ham. Add remainder of cheese. In bowl whisk flour, milk, eggs and parsley. Pour in pan on top of other ingredients. Bake 35-45 minutes at 350 degrees. Serves 12, 130 cal., 25 g protein.

Forget the Diet Rolls
Lois Corl

4 cups self-rising flour
16 oz. sour cream
4 sticks Land of Lakes Country Morning Butter

Preheat oven to 400 degrees. Mix sour cream and soft butter. Gently add flour like you would biscuits until blended. Do not overwork dough. Pinch off and gently roll between your hands or drop by spoonfuls walnut sized pieces of dough and place in mini muffin pans. Bake for 15 minutes. These are best right out of the oven. This recipe makes quite a few. I like to bake a pan or two at a time through dinner. Too good!!!

Fruit & Nut Quick Bread
Pam Herrington

1 1/2 cups whole wheat flour
1/2 cup brown sugar
1 1/2 tsp. cinnamon
1 cup chopped pitted prunes
2 Tbsp. chopped pecans or walnuts
1 tsp. baking soda
1 cup nonfat milk
1 egg white (slightly beaten)

Mix flour, sugar, cinnamon, prunes and pecans. Set aside. Stir soda into milk. Add egg white. Stir mixture into dry ingredients. Pour into nonstick bread pan and let stand for 20 minutes. Bake at 350 F for 50 minutes. Cool bread in pan on cooling rack. Remove from pan when cool. Serves 16.

Gingerbread Pancakes
Becky Wessel

2 1/4 cup flour
1 1/2 tsp. baking powder
1 1/2 tsp. soda
1/2 tsp. salt
1 tsp. cinnamon
1 tsp. ginger
1 tsp. nutmeg
1/2 tsp. cloves
1 egg
3/4 cup buttermilk
3/4 cup water
1/4 cup melted butter
1/4 cup brown sugar

Mix ingredients. Pour onto buttered griddle in 4 inch circles. Flip so each side is golden brown. Serve hot with whipped cream.

Golden Nugget Biscuits
Lorraine DelValle/Stacy Metz

4 cups self-rising flour sifted
3/4 cup shortening
1 1/4 cups milk or buttermilk

In large bowl add flour - make a well in center. Add shortening and milk. Squeeze shortening into small pieces with fingers. Gradually work in flour until batter is just firm. Do NOT over mix! Then roll into 1/2 inch thick and cut or pinch off large ball and roll in palm, until smooth. Place on greased cookie sheet and press tops gently. Bake at 425 for approx. 20-25 min.

Larry's Pancakes
Larry Wise

1 1/2 cups flour
1 Tbsp. baking powder
1/4 tsp. baking soda
2 cups buttermilk
1 Tbsp. brown sugar
1 tsp. salt
3 eggs
1/4 cup oil

Put dry ingredients in mixing bowl. Separate 3 egg yolks and put with dry ingredients. Whip whites in separate bowl until stiff. Add buttermilk and oil into dry ingredients. Mix ingredients slowly only until uniformly wet. Fold in egg whites. Fry on griddle using only small amount of oil. Drop a few blueberries into frying pancakes before turning them over. ENJOY!!! Larry often doubles this recipe and uses it for waffles the next day.

Lime Nut Bread
Sandy Taylor

Bread
1 cup sugar
3 eggs
2 tsp. baking powder
2/3 cup milk
1/2 cup butter softened
2 1/2 cup flour
1 tsp. salt
2 Tbsp. fresh, Florida lime juice
1 Tbsp. fresh, grated Florida lime peel
3/4 cup chopped pecans

Lime Glaze
1 cup sifted powdered sugar   4 tsp. fresh, Florida lime juice

In a large bowl, with electric mixer, beat together sugar and butter. Add eggs, one at a time, beating well after each addition. In a separate bowl, combine flour, baking powder and salt and stir to combine. Add flour mixture to egg mixture alternately with milk. Beat in lime juice and peel; stir in pecans. Pour into greased 9x5x3 inch loaf pan and bake at 350F., 50-60 minutes or until toothpick inserted near center comes out clean. Cool in pan 10 minutes; remove from pan and finish cooling on wire rack. Drizzle with lime glaze. Slice thinly to serve. Makes 1 loaf lime glaze Combine powdered sugar and lime juice; mix well.

Pancake Mix
Heather Boswell

1 1/2 cups flour
2 tsp. baking powder
3/4 tsp. salt
2 eggs
2 Tbsp. oil
1 1/2 cup milk or more.

Mix all ingredients together. This is a base mix but you can add berries, bananas, etc.

Poppy Seed Bread
Bonnie Swete

1 lemon cake mix
1 box lemon instant pudding
1 cup of hot water
1/2 cup of oil
1/4 cup poppy seeds

Combine and beat all ingredients in a bowl for 4 minutes. Pour mix into 2 greased bread pans. Bake at 350 degrees for 45-50 minutes. Recipe makes two loaves.

Quick & Easy Pimento Cheese Sandwiches
Angela Dyches

1 pkg. of crumbled cheddar cheese
1 4-oz. jar of pimentos
1/2 cup of mayonnaise
2 Tbsp. of dry sherry

Mix all four ingredients together. This is best if allowed to sit over night. Makes 4 sandwiches.

Raisin Soy Bread
Whitney Lavoie

1 1/4 cups soy milk
1 1/2 tsp. salt
2 Tbsp. honey
2 Tbsp. butter, softened
2 cups bread flour
1 cup whole wheat flour
1 cup soy flour
2 tsp. ground cinnamon
1 cup raisins
2 1/4 tsp. active dry yeast

Place ingredients in the pan of the bread machine in the order recommended by the manufacturer. Select basic bread setting, light/medium crust setting; press Start. If your machine has a Fruit setting, add the raisins at the signal, or about 5 minutes before the kneading cycle has finished.

Sausage Breakfast Casserole
Janice Sprowles

6 slices bread
3 Tbsp. butter or margarine
1 lb. pork sausage
2 cups grated cheddar cheese
6 eggs, beaten
2 cup whole milk
1 tsp. salt

Remove crusts from bread; spread bread slices with butter. Place in greased 13x9x2 inch baking dish. Cook sausage until browned, stirring to crumble; drain well. Spoon sausage over bread; sprinkle with cheese. Combine remaining ingredients; mix well and pour over cheese. Cover casserole and chill overnight. Remove from refrigerator 15 minutes before baking. Bake, uncovered, at 350 degrees for 40 minutes or until set.

Sausage Casserole
Elizabeth Linzy

1 lb. sausage, mild or hot cooked & drained
2/3 cup chopped celery
2/3 cup chopped onion
2/3 cup chopped green pepper
1 cup rice, uncooked
1 can cream of chicken soup
1 can water

Sauté celery, onion & green pepper. Place cooked sausage on bottom of casserole dish. Add vegetables. Mix rice, soup & water. Pour over top, Cover with foil. Bake 350 for 40-45 minutes.

Sausage Oven Pancake Squares
Judy Daniels

1 12 oz. bulk pork sausage
1 cup shredded cheddar cheese
1 egg
1/4 cup milk
2 Tbsp. maple syrup
1 Tbsp. vegetable oil
1/2 cup all purpose flour
1 Tbsp. baking powder
1/8 Tsp salt
3/4 cup maple syrup (for topping)

Heat oven to 350. In 10-inch skillet, cook sausage over medium heat, until no longer pink. Drain sausage. In ungreased 8x8 or 9x9 square pan, spread sausage. Sprinkle with cheese. In large bowl, beat egg, milk, syrup and oil with a wire whisk until well blended. Beat in flour, baking powder and salt. Pour batter evenly over sausage and cheese. Bake uncovered 25-30 minutes or until golden brown. Serve topped with 3/4 cup maple syrup.

Scones
Linda Rehder

In large bowl mix :
3 cups unbleached flour (sifted)
1 Tbsp. baking powder
1 tsp. salt
3/4 cup white sugar

Add your choice:
Craisins, nuts, dried apricots, raisins or dried mango
Grate: 1 stick REAL butter into flour mixture and stir with wood spoon
Stir in: 1 cup real heavy cream or half and half (I use fat free Half and Half Add: 1 Tbsp of your choice: almond flavoring, vanilla, or orange juice (if use OJ also add orange rind zest)

Lightly knead dough on floured surface. Roll out 1 inch thickness circle. Cut like a pizza in wedges or use a large circle cutter. Put on baking sheet, brush with cream, Half & Half or milk and sprinkle with sugar. Bake at 425 degrees for approximately 15-17 minutes.

Seasoned Swirl Rolls
Pam Herrington

24 Rhodes Texas Rolls, thawed but still cold (any raw rolls chilled)
1 Tbsp. seasoning blend
1 Tbsp. dried oregano
1 Tbsp. dried basil
1/4 cup grated parmesan cheese
1/4 cup butter, melted

Combine seasoning blend, herbs and cheese. Roll each roll into a 12-inch rope and brush with butter to completely coat. Sprinkle one side with herb mixture. Form rope into a coil, seasoned side in. Place in a muffin tin sprayed with non-stick cooking spray. Cover with sprayed plastic wrap and let rise until double in size. Remove wrap and bake at 350 degrees for 15-20 minutes.

Six week Bran Muffins
Durst Family

1 15 oz. box raisin bran
1 1/4 cup brown sugar
5 tsp. baking soda
4 eggs, beaten
1 cup oil

1 1/4 cup white sugar
5 cups flour
2 tsp. salt
1 qt buttermilk

Combine all ingredients in a large (5 quart size) bowl with cover. Mix well. Fill muffin cups 2/3 full. Bake at 400 degrees for 15 minutes. Refrigerate dough in covered container for up to 6 weeks. Use batter as needed. Makes 5-6 dozen.

Zucchini Bread
Pam Herrington

3 eggs
2 cups flour
1 tsp. salt
2 cup sugar
2 tsp. soda
1 cup chopped walnuts (optional)

1 cup oil
1/4 tsp. baking powder
3 tsp. vanilla
2 cup zucchini - grated
3 tsp. cinnamon
1 cup raisins

Beat eggs. Add sugar, oil & zucchini. Sift flour and dry ingredients. Mix walnuts and raisins with all ingredients. Put in two loaf pans. Bake at 350 for one hour.

Vegetables and Side Dishes

"And God said, "Look! I have given you the seed-bearing plants throughout the earth and all the fruit trees for your food."
Genesis 1:29

Vegetables and Side Dishes

Baked Mac & Cheese
Heather Boswell

1 8 oz. package macaroni
2 Tbsp. butter
2 Tbsp. all purpose flour
2 cups milk
1/2 tsp. salt
1/2 tsp. pepper
1 8 oz. block sharp cheddar, shredded and divided

Prepare pasta/keep warm. Melt butter on med. low heat. Whisk in flour, until smooth. Cook, whisking constantly for 2 mins. Gradually whisk in milk cook, whisking constantly for 5 mins. or until thickened. Remove from heat. Stir in salt, pepper, and 1 cup cheese and the pasta. Spoon pasta into a lightly greased 2 quart baking dish. Top with rest of cheese. Bake at 400 for 20 mins. Let stand for 10 mins. before serving.

Barbecued Kidney Beans
Kate Schau

Large can of kidney beans (48 oz.)
8 oz. can tomato sauce
2-3 cups sliced apples (do not peel)
1/2 lb. of bacon (optional)
2 cups sliced onion
1/2 cup brown sugar

Mix all ingredients well and bake at 350 degrees for 1 & 1/2 to 3 hours. (Cover if desired with foil for the first hour.) Serves 10-12 people.

BBQ Green Beans
Andy Botts

1 lb. of green beans (cut, and drained)
1 can of tomato soup
1 large onion
6 slices of bacon (I prefer turkey bacon)
1/2 cup of brown sugar
1 cup of ketchup
1 can of French's Crispy Fried Onions

Cut up the bacon and the onion into small pieces. Sauté the onion and bacon, with butter in a medium skillet. Mix the tomato soup, ketchup, and brown sugar, then pour over bacon and onions. Pour entire mixture over green beans in a casserole dish. Bake at 350 degrees for 25 minutes Take out, put crispy onions on top, and put back in the oven for 5 more minutes, or until bubbling on top.

Broccoli Casserole
Lynn Francisco

2 pkg. chopped broccoli (thawed and uncooked)
1 can cream of mushroom
1 small can of mushrooms
6 slices of American cheese
Oleo
Pepperidge Farm Stuffing

Put in 2 qt. greased casserole in 4 layers (broccoli, soup, mushrooms and cheese) and top with the following: Heat 2 cups water and 1/3 cup oleo until melted. Add 2 cups Pepperidge Farm stuffing, toss lightly and put on top - cover with paprika. Bake uncovered at 325 degrees - 45 minutes or until bubbly.

Carrot Loaf
Linda Rehder

1 ½ cups cooked carrots
1 cup dried bread crumbs
1 tsp. salt
½ tsp. pepper
1 tsp. minced onions
1 cup half and half
3 well beaten eggs
2 Tbsp. melted butter or margarine
1 Tbsp. sugar

Mash cooked carrots. Add remaining ingredients in order. Place in a very well greased loaf pan or ring mold pan. Bake at 350 degrees, 45 to 60 min. until well set. May line pan with well greased waxed paper for easier removal. Remove from oven when loaf is set in middle and let set 10 min. before removing. Turn loaf upside down on a decorative dish. May surround cooked frozen peas or if you used a ring mold, add peas to the center opening. A favorite holiday recipe.

Calico Beans
Carla Kelly

1/2 lb. bacon
1/8 cup onion
1 can pork and beans
1 small can lima beans
1/3 cup brown sugar
2 tsp. vinegar
1/2 lb. hamburger
1/2 cup catsup
1 can kidney beans
3/4 tsp. salt
1 tsp. mustard

Brown bacon, hamburger, and onion. Drain fat. Put bacon, burger, onion, catsup, beans (undrained), salt, brown sugar, mustard and vinegar into crock pot. Simmer 1 hour.

Cheese Grits
Tom, Debi, and Kathy Jo Cole

4 cups water
1 cup quick grits
1 stick butter
1/4 lb. cheddar cheese, shredded
2 eggs
1/4 cup milk

Bring water and grits to a boil. Add eggs and stir rapidly to separate. Add 1/2 of the cheese. When cheese is dissolved, pour into a 9x13 inch baking dish. Sprinkle remaining cheese over top. Bake 45 minutes to 1 hour at 400 degrees. Let set 20 to 30 minutes before it is served.

Cheesy Macaroni and Cheese
Julia Baron

2 cups Muellers elbow macaroni
1/4 cup butter
2 1/2 Tbsp. flour
1/8 tsp. dry mustard
1/8 tsp. salt
1/8 tsp. white pepper
2 cups milk
2 cups sharp cheddar cheese, shredded
2 cups Monterey jack cheese, shredded

Cook macaroni for 3 minutes in boiling water. Drain and put aside. In large sauce pan melt butter, add flour, mustard, salt and pepper. Add milk, bring to boil stirring constantly. Stir in 3 cups cheese leaving 1 cup for top. Stir in cooked macaroni, pour into 2 quart casserole dish top with remaining cup of cheese. Bake 350 for 25-30 minutes. ENJOY!!

Cheesy Mac N' Cheese
Megan Johnson

1 Tbsp. vegetable oil
1 lb. macaroni 1 stick + 1 tablespoon butter
1/2 cup shredded muenster
1/2 cup cheddar, shredded
1/2 cup sharp cheddar, shredded
1/2 cup Monterey jack, shredded
2 cups half and half
1 cup Velveeta (cut in small cubes)
2 large eggs (slightly beaten)
1/4 tsp. salt
1/8 tsp. pepper

Heat oven to 350 degrees. Butter 2 1/2 quart casserole dish with tablespoon of butter. Cook macaroni with oil until tender (about 7 min.), melt 1 stick of butter in pan and stir in macaroni, mix shredded cheeses. Add half and half to macaroni. Combine 1 1/2 cups shredded cheese, cubed Velveeta, eggs. Add salt and pepper (stir). Put in casserole dish, add remaining cheese on top. Bake 35 minutes.

Cheesy Potato Casserole
Patty Phillips

2 packages frozen hash browns (cubed and Spanish style are the best)
8 oz. sour cream
1 can cream of chicken soup
8 oz. cheddar cheese, shredded

Mix well. Place in 9x13 pan. Bake 35-40 minutes at 350 degrees. Great any time any meal but really great for large crowds and buffets.

Chinese Carrots
Megan Johnson

2 pounds carrots
1 can tomato soup
1 cup sugar
1 large bell pepper

1 cup oil
1/2 cup white vinegar
1 large onion

Cut carrots into one inch slices and cook (do not overcook). Combine oil, soup, vinegar and sugar in a bowl. Cut onion and bell pepper. Add oil mixture to carrots, along with onion and bell pepper. Simmer until onion and pepper are soften (do not overcook).

Corn Casserole
Roberta Boyd/Ashlie Fulmer

1 can whole kernel corn (14-15 ounces)
1 can cream style corn (14-15 ounces)
1 cup sour cream
1 stick of butter melted
1 box Jiffy Corn Muffin Mix
1 egg

So easy and tastes great. Grease a 13x9 pan. Set a side. Heat oven to 350 degrees. Mix all ingredients together. Pour into greased pan and cook for 45-50 minutes or until top is lightly brown.

Corn Pudding
Lorraine DelValle/Stacy Metz

1 can whole kernel corn, 1/2 drained
1 can creamed corn
1 box Jiffy Corn Muffin Mix
1/2 cup cooking oil

8 oz. sour cream
1/3 cup sugar
2 eggs

Combine all ingredients. Bake at 350 for 30 minutes or until set and lightly browned, in casserole dish.

Corn Pudding
Tina Yoder

4 cans corn (17 oz. can)
1 cup milk
1 cup sugar
3 tsp. flour
3 eggs
salt to taste
1/2 stick of butter

Combine all ingredients, but the butter. Pour into a large buttered casserole dish. Dot with butter. Bake uncovered at 350 for 1 hour.

Creamed Spinach
Julia Baron

1 cup milk
1/4 cup butter
1/4 cup flour
1 10 oz. bag chopped frozen spinach

In medium sauté pan melt butter. When bubbling, whisk in flour. Cook on medium-low heat 1 minute, slowly whisk in milk. Add frozen spinach. Cover and cook 3-5 minutes. Salt and pepper to taste.

Dad's Thanksgiving Dressing
Lois Corl

3 loaves Pepperidge Farm Bread - original recipe ("day old" is best)
4 sticks butter
3-4 medium to large onions, diced
6-8 large stalks of celery with lots of leaves diced
3-4 chicken bouillon cubes
3 cans of soup any combination (Cream of Celery, Chicken, or Mushroom)
1 1/2 tsp. of sage
2 tsp. of thyme
1/4 tsp. of pepper
1 tsp. of poultry seasoning

The day before Thanksgiving cut bread into half inch cubes. This was Dad's favorite part. He loved it. Occasionally he would let one of us do it. You will get two big bowls full. Keep uncovered and toss periodically to dry out. (putting it in the refrigerator uncovered works too.) The goal is for bread cubes that are dried out on the outside but moist on the inside. I know you can buy crouton-like bread cubes, but it isn't the same. The next day or when bread is ready: Preheat oven to 325 degrees. Melt butter in large frying pan. Sauté diced onions and celery with leaves until tender crisp. Add bouillon cubes, soup and spices and stir until blended. Simmer for a little while to blend flavors. Put all of your bread crumbs into a large bowl. I use my big black roasting pan. Pour mixture onto bread cubes and toss well. At this point you have two options: Place in two buttered 9x13 pans and cook covered with foil for 30 minutes and then cook uncovered for 15 more minutes until brown and crispy on top. For a fancy presentation: Form into serving sized balls and either wrap each one in Saran Wrap and freeze until needed or cook on cookie sheet or shallow pan with a pecan on top of each ball until cooked through and brown and crispy on outside. Usually about 30 minutes. This was the way Banks' mom would make dressing (with a different recipe.) I love doing it this way to combine family traditions. I usually cook what I need and then freeze the rest for another meal.

Everyone's Favorite Baked Beans
Kelly Beale

1 med chopped onion	1 lb. baked beans (not drained)
1 lb. kidney beans (drained)	1 lb. lima beans (drained)
1/4 cup grated sharp cheddar cheese	1/2 cup brown sugar
1 Tbsp. Worcestershire sauce	1/3 cup ketchup
Grated parmesan cheese	

Preheat the oven to 350. Sauté onions until lightly golden then combine all the ingredients together in a dish - all but the parmesan cheese. Bake for 30 min. then sprinkle the parmesan cheese over the top and bake another 15 min.

Fancy Green Beans
Pam Herrington

2 Tbsp. teriyaki sauce	1 Tbsp. honey
1 Tbsp. butter	1 Tbsp. fresh lemon juice
1 1/2 lbs. fresh green beans	2 slices bacon
1/2 cup red bell pepper, strips	1/2 cup thin onion wedges
1/2 cup whole cashews	

In a small bowl, stir together the teriyaki sauce, honey, and butter. Fill a bowl with cold water and ice cubes. Bring a large pot of water to a boil and add the lemon juice. Drop in the beans and cook for 4 to 5 minutes or until beans are bright green. Drain the beans in a colander and then plunge them into the iced water. Drain again and set aside. In a skillet, cook the bacon until very crispy, crumble and set aside. Sauté the bell pepper and onion in the hot bacon fat for 2 minutes. Add the beans, cashews and bacon to the skillet. Add the teriyaki-honey sauce and toss gently.

Garlic Potatoes
Jannon Pierce

1/2 cup oil
2 Tbsp. parmesan cheese
1 tsp. salt
1/2 tsp. garlic powder
1/2 paprika
1/4 tsp. pepper
2-4 potatoes

Mix all ingredients except potatoes. Clean potatoes and cut up so that skin is on each wedge. Place wedges in a Pyrex, coat with mixture. Bake on 350 for 1 hour or until potatoes are done.

Gingered Spaghetti Squash
Pam Herrington

1 small spaghetti squash (cut in half & deseed)
2 Tbsp. butter
1 Tbsp. honey
1/2 Tbsp. minced ginger
Salt and pepper, to taste

Preheat oven to 375. Place squash on baking dish. Add the butter, honey, ginger and seasoning. Bake for 45-60 minutes - until al dente. Do not overcook. Spoon out squash and check for seasoning. Keep warm for serving.

Grandma's Cornbread Dressing
Lee Ann Martin

1 pan fresh cornbread made with 3 eggs.
(it is important that you do not use left over cornbread)
3 slices white bread
6 crushed saltine crackers
1 medium onion, chopped
2 stalks celery, chopped
1 tsp. sage
3 boiled eggs, chopped
3 raw eggs
1 can cream of chicken soup
1 can cream of celery soup
Chicken broth
Salt and pepper, to taste

Mix cornbread with bread torn into small pieces. Add all remaining ingredients except broth. Mix well. Add enough chicken broth to make a very wet mixture (usually about 1/2 can). Mix well and refrigerate overnight, if possible. Bake in a greased pan 450 degrees until brown (about 30 min.).

Green Bean Bundles
Andreah Wellman

2 cans whole green beans
1/4 cup Worcestershire sauce
3/4 cup brown sugar
Salt, pepper, garlic powder...to taste

1/2 cup butter, (melted)
3/4 lb. bacon

Put about 10 beans per bundle. Wrap a piece of bacon around each bundle. Secure with a toothpick. Melt butter in saucepan. Add brown sugar and Worcestershire sauce. Pour over green bean bundles in a 9x13" dish. Season with salt, pepper, and garlic powder to taste. Bake at 375 for 20-30 min.

Grits Casserole
Sally Humphries

1 cup grits
1/2 tsp. salt
4 beaten eggs
3 cup boiling water
1/4 cup cheddar cheese
1/2 stick butter
1 cup milk

Pour grits in boiling water, mix well, and cook well. Add remaining ingredients. Stir thoroughly. Place in casserole. Bake at 350 for 30 minutes. Enjoy!

Homemade Mac and Feta Cheese
Patty Phillips

13-15 oz. elbow macaroni
8 Tbsp. melted butter
1-2 cups shredded parmesan cheese
Salt and pepper to taste
1 egg
2 cups milk
4-5 cups feta cheese

Heat oven to 350 degrees. Lightly grease a 9x13 backing dish. Lightly boil macaroni (about half cooked). Whisk egg, milk, butter and salt and pepper. Add cheese to mixture and stir well. Add cooked macaroni and mix. Press mixture into pan. Bake uncovered for 30-40 minutes. Can be made in advance and put into refrigerator just let sit on counter 15 minutes prior to cooling. If you are serving a large group better make 2 **** it goes fast****

Mom's Corn Pudding
Megan Johnson

5 eggs
1 (15.25 oz.) can whole kernel corn
1/2 cup milk
2 (14.75 oz.) cans of cream style corn

1/3 cup melted butter
1/4 cup white sugar
4 Tbsp. corn starch

Heat oven to 400 degrees. Grease a 2 qt. casserole dish. Lightly, beat eggs. Add butter, sugar, milk. Whisk in starch. Stir in corn. Blend ingredients, pour into dish and bake 1 hour.

Potato Casserole
Sharon Schroeter

1 lrg. bag frozen hash browns [cubes]
1 can cream of mushroom soup
1 can cream of celery soup
1 cup shredded cheddar cheese
1 cup sour cream
1 Tbsp. dried chives

Mix all ingredients together in a 9x13 or similar baking dish. Bake at 325 for 1-1/2 hrs or 350 for 1 hour.

Sausage Bake Beans
Pam McFarland

1 lb. ground sausage
1 small green pepper
1/2 cup ketchup
1/2 tsp. salt
1 tsp. Worcestershire Sauce

2 27 oz. pork and beans
1 small onion, chopped
1/2 cup brown sugar
1 tsp. mustard

Cook sausage and drain. Mix in large bowl all other ingredients. Add sausage. Spray 9x11. Spry pan with Pam. Pour contents in pan. Do not cover. Bake 350 degrees for 45 minutes.

Scalloped Corn
Linda Rehder

3 cups frozen or fresh corn, cooked (or 3 cans of canned corn)
2 sticks margarine or butter (divided, see instructions)
2 cans creamed corn   1 cup diced celery
1/2 cup chopped onion   1/3 cup flour
2 Tbsp. sugar   3 eggs, well beaten
1 cup Half and Half (or milk)   1 tsp. black pepper
1 tsp. salt   1 tsp. celery salt
1/2 tsp. paprika   2 Tbsp. lemon juice
2 cups dried bread cubed (5-6 pieces of bread)
2/3 cup parmesan cheese

Melt 1 stick of margarine in sauce pan. Add chopped celery and onion and cook until tender. In large casserole dish add: corn, cooked celery and onion, beaten eggs, flour, salt, pepper, celery salt, paprika, sugar & lemon juice. Add half and half last. Stir these ingredients well. Bake at 375 degrees for 1 hour or until center is set. In microwave safe bowl place second stick of margarine and melt in microwave. Add parmesan cheese and stir. Fold in cubed dried bread crumbs. Stir until bread is covered with butter mixture. Place bread mixture over cooked scalloped corn. Place back in oven for another 15-20 minutes until bread is toasted (watch carefully).

Sinful Potatoes
Pam Herrington

2 lbs hash brown potatoes, thawed   1/2 cup margarine, melted
1 tsp. salt   1/4 tsp. pepper
10 oz. shredded mozzarella cheese   1 pt. sour cream
1/2 cup chopped onion
1 can cream of chicken or mushroom soup
1 small can mushrooms or fresh mushrooms
Topping: 2 cups cornflakes, crushed 1/2 cup margarine – melted

Mix all of your ingredients (except the cornflakes and 1/2 cup margarine) and place in a 9x13 inch pan. Top with the cornflakes and 1/2 cup margarine. Bake at 350 for 1 1/2 hours.

Spaghetti Squash with Parmesan Cheese
Pam Herrington

1 medium spaghetti squash
1/2 cup grated parmesan cheese
1/2 stick butter
Salt and pepper, to taste

Use a paring knife to prick squash all over. Place in a baking dish and bake 1 hour or until soft. Cut squash in half. Scoop out and discard seeds. Using a fork, scrap flesh in strings into a serving bowl. Toss with parmesan cheese and butter. Season to taste with salt and pepper.

Squash Casserole
Pam Herrington

8 cup yellow summer squash
1/2 cup water
1/2 tsp. garlic salt
1 cup onion diced
8 oz. cream cheese
1/2 tsp. dill weed

Cook squash, onion & water together for 5 minutes then drain. Mix cream cheese, garlic salt & dill weed with above while hot. Place all in casserole and put buttered crumbs on top. (I use flavored croutons crushed on top) and bake ½ hour at 350.

Sweet Potato Casserole
Heather Boswell

3 cups sweet potatoes (about 6-8 fresh) 1/2 cup sugar
1 tsp. vanilla   1/2 cup milk
2 eggs   2/3 cup butter (softened)
1/2 cup flour   1 cup brown sugar
Bag of mini marshmallows

Peel sweet potatoes and chop into chunks. Boil until tender, drain and let cool. Mash. While mashing, add 1/3 cup butter, 1/2 cup sugar, 1 tsp vanilla, 1/2 cup milk, and 2 eggs. Mix together. Pour into baking dish. In a separate bowl, mix 1/3 cup butter, 1/2 cup flour, and 1 cup brown sugar. Mix and sprinkle over top of potato mixture. Bake at 350 for 35 min. Remove from oven. Sprinkle marshmallows on top then put back in oven until marshmallows have melted.

Sweet Potato Casserole
Jean McIntyre

2 40 oz. can of sweet potatoes (drained and mashed)
2 eggs   1 cup of brown sugar
1 tsp. vanilla   1/2 tsp. salt
1/2 cup milk   1/2 stick of butter

TOPPING:
1 cup of brown sugar   1 cup of pecans
1/3 cup of all purpose flour   1/2 stick of butter

Preheat oven to 350. Mix all ingredients together and put in a glass baking dish (9X12). Topping: Mix dry ingredients together, then add melted butter and pecans. Sprinkle on top. Baked uncovered for 30 minutes. Enjoy!

Sweet Potato Soufflé
Linda Rehder

Soufflé Ingredients:
4 large sweet potatoes peeled and cooked
3/4 cups milk or half and half   1 tsp. vanilla
1/4 cup sugar   1/4 cup brown sugar
3 eggs   6 Tbsp. melted butter or margarine

Topping Ingredients:
6 Tbsp. melted butter or margarine
1/2 cup finely chopped Pecans   1/2 cup brown sugar
3/4 cups crushed bran flakes (add these last)

Preheat oven at 350 degrees. Mash cooked potatoes then add remaining soufflé ingredients. Bake in 2 quart baking dish for 40-60 min. or until edges pull away from sides and center is set like a pumpkin pie. Remove from oven and sprinkle topping evenly over soufflé mixture. Put under boiler and watch VERY carefully until slightly toasted.

Susan's Corn and Macaroni Casserole
Kim Barger

1 (14 ¾ oz.) can cream corn
1 can whole corn, do not drain
3/4 stick margarine, melted
1 cup macaroni, uncooked
1 Tbsp. diced onion
1 cup diced or shredded Velveeta cheese

Combine all ingredients in bowl and stir lightly. Pour into 1 ½ quart casserole dish. Cover and bake at 350 degrees for 30 minutes, then bake uncovered for 30 more minutes.

Twice Baked Potato Casserole
Angela Dyches

8 med baking potatoes (may substitute red)
2 cups of shredded cheddar cheese, divided (8 oz.)
1 16 oz. container of sour cream
1 8 oz. package of cream cheese
1/2 cup milk
1/2 cup of butter or margarine, melted
2 garlic cloves, minced
1 Tbsp. of chopped fresh chives
1 1/2 tsp. of salt
1/2 tsp. of pepper
6 bacon slices, cooked and crumbled
4 green onions, chopped
1/4 cup chopped fresh chives

Bake potatoes in oven until done. Scoop out potato into a large bowl. Add 1 cup of cheddar cheese and the next 8 ingredients. Spoon mixture into a lightly greased 13x9 inch baking pan. Bake at 350 for 30 minutes or until thorough heated. It should be bubbly. Sprinkle remaining 1 cup of cheese, bacon, green onions and chives over the top. It may need to go back in the oven for another 5-10 minutes to melt toppings.
Serves 8.

Tex-Mex Bean Salad
Georgie Mygrant

2 cans of kidney beans (drained and rinsed)
1 can of corn (drained)
1 can of white beans (drained and rinsed)
1 cup of cooked whole wheat macaroni (drained)
1 med. size jar of salsa (hot, medium, or mild)
1/2 cup of shredded lite cheese
If you like it hot, you can add 1/4 cup of hot peppers.

Mix gently the beans and corn. Fold in the macaroni and the salsa. Pour into a bowl, and sprinkle cheese over the top. This dish is very low in calories and fat. Plus the beans are high in fiber, and also helps lower your cholesterol. So, eat with no guilt, and enjoy!

Soups and Salads

"And the Lord God made all kinds of trees grow out of the ground--trees that are pleasing to the eye and good for food..."
Genesis 2:9

Soups and Salads

Apple Salad
Carol Williams

4 cups apples (cubed)
½ cup raisins
1 cup crushed pineapple (drained)
½ cup tiny marshmallows
¼ cup sugar
¾ cup mayonnaise

Mix all the above except mayonnaise. Stir this in just before serving.

Apricot Salad
Lita Murtha

1 20 oz. can crushed pineapple (not drained)
2 small packages apricot jello
2 cups buttermilk
1 12 oz. carton Cool Whip

Bring pineapple to a boil. Remove from heat, add jello. Cool. Add buttermilk and Cool Whip. Mix well and refrigerate in 9x9 dish.

Benevento Bread Salad
Mindy Cress

1 large load of day old bread, chopped (the harder/the better)
1 roasted red pepper (jar works great, drain liquid)
2 large tomatoes, chopped
2 cups extra virgin olive oil
1/2 cup red wine vinegar
1 small red onion, finely chopped
mini mozzarella balls (as many as you like)

Chop bread into 1/2 inch cubes and place in large bowl. Toss with remaining ingredients and serve chilled. *Makes a great side dish for fish.

Broccoli Cheese Soup
Linda Rehder

2 large bunches of fresh broccoli, washed and cut
2 cans cream of chicken soup
1 lb. Velveeta cheese cut in chunks
1 quart Half and Half (I use fat free Half and Half)
2 cups milk
1 tsp. salt
1 tsp. black pepper
2 tsp. celery salt
6 Tbsp. butter
1 cup instant mashed potato buds (use more if needed to thicken)

Cook broccoli in small amount of water until tender. Do not drain. Add: soup, cheese, salt, celery salt, pepper and butter. Stir constantly over low heat until cheese is melted. Add Half & Half and milk. When soup returns to warm status add instant mashed potatoes to thicken soup. Sir frequently over low heat until hot (but do NOT boil). Add more instant potatoes as needed to desired thickness.

Broccoli Salad
Sylvia Kursawe

1 head fresh broccoli, cut into bite size pieces
1/4 cup red onion, chopped
1/2 cup raisins
3 Tbsp. white wine vinegar
2 Tbsp. white sugar
1 cup mayonnaise
1 cup sunflower seeds

In a medium bowl, combine the broccoli, onion and raisins. In a small bowl, whisk together the vinegar, sugar and mayonnaise. Pour over broccoli mixture, and toss until well mixed. Refrigerate for at least two hours. Before serving, toss salad with crumbled bacon and sunflower seeds.

Broccoli Salad
Lynn Francisco (In memory of Cindy Francisco)

3 stems of broccoli
1 medium onion, chopped
1 cup mozzarella cheese

6-8 slices of cooked bacon
3-4 boiled eggs

Dressing: 1 cup Hellman's mayonnaise,, 1/2 cup sugar 14 cup vinegar
SHAKE WELL IN JAR OR CONTAINER
Chop broccoli (I use heads only) Crumble bacon Add dressing when ready to serve

Broccoli Salad
Sheila Mathis

1 bunch fresh broccoli, washed and cut up
1 cup shredded cheddar cheese
1 lb. bacon, cooked and chopped fine
1/2 cup chopped onion

Sauce: 3/4 cup mayonnaise 2 Tbsp. white vinegar 2 Tbsp. sugar

Mix sauce ingredients. Toss sauce with other ingredients and chill in refrigerator for one hour.

Broccoli and Cauliflower Salad
Katrina West

1/2 lb. cooked bacon
1 bag broccoli
2 tsp. apple cider vinegar
1 med red onion finely, chopped
1 bag cauliflower
1/2 cup sunflower seeds
1/2 cup raisins
1/2 cup mayonnaise

Prepare in large skillet bacon and fry until crisp. Drain on a paper towel, crumble and set aside. In large bowl, combine broccoli, cauliflower, raisins, sunflower seeds and red onion. In small bowl, stir together mayonnaise, sugar and vinegar. Spoon over broccoli mixture; toss to coat. Sprinkle bacon over salad and toss. Cover and refrigerate 3 hours or overnight.

Broccoli Salad - Weight Watchers
Pam Herrington

3 cups Broccoli & or Cauliflower.
1 medium onion, chopped
3 Tbsp. bacon bits
¾ cup cheddar cheese
¼ cup sweetener
1/3 cup lite mayonnaise
¼ cup apple cider vinegar

Mix sweetener, mayonnaise and vinegar. Pour on broccoli, onion, bacon & cheese. Mix all and refrigerate 2 to 3 hours.

Brunswick Stew
Elizabeth Linzy

1 4 pound chicken
2 1/2 quarts water
2 Tbsp. salt
1 or 2 stalks celery, chopped
1/2 cup onion, chopped
2 1/2 cups canned tomatoes, chopped
1 1/2 cups lima beans
2 cups whole kernel corn
1/4 tsp. black pepper
2 tsp. Worcestershire sauce
1 cup sifted flour

Cut chicken in pieces. Place in heavy saucepan. Add water, salt and celery. Cook about 1 1/2 hours or until tender, but not falling off the bones. Remove chicken from bones. Discard skin. Cut in generous sized pieces and return to broth. Add onions, tomatoes, beans, corn, pepper and Worcestershire sauce. Blend thoroughly. While this cooks, make a gravy thickening by adding sufficient water to the flour to make a smooth paste. Slowly add to stew, stirring constantly. Cook until desired thickening is reached.

Carrot Salad
Carol Williams

4 cups shredded carrots
1/4 cup sugar
1/2 cup raisins
2 Tbsp. frozen orange juice
1 cup crushed pineapple (drained)
1/2 cup mayonnaise

Mix all the above except mayonnaise. Stir this in just before serving. If desired, add more mayonnaise, depending on liquid from juices. If it seems to moist, drain off some before adding mayonnaise.

Caldo Gallego/Spanish Galician Soup
Dick & Gertrude Garland

3 cans white northern beans
4 cans chicken broth
1 package chorizo sausage
1 onion, chopped
8 oz. frozen chopped collard greens
4 medium potatoes, chopped
Chopped ham or salt pork
Salt & pepper to taste

Remove casing, crumble and cook chorizo sausage in large skillet. If using cooked sausage, remove casing and crumble. Cook cubed potatoes and one can of chicken broth in medium pan until they begin to soften. Combine beans, chicken broth, chopped onion, cooked potatoes and broth, sausage, chopped ham or salt pork, and chopped collards in large pot. Cook on stove for about 20 minutes. Transfer to crock pot and cook for about 4 hours. (Can be simmered longer in crock pot.)

Carrot Soup
Becky Wessel

3 Tbsp. butter
7 large coarsely chopped carrots
1 cup sliced celery
1/2 tsp. salt
3/4 cup chopped onion
2 medium sized diced potatoes
32 oz. chicken broth

Melt butter in large pan. Add and sauté onions and celery until soft. Add chicken broth and 1/2 tsp salt and bring to boil. Add carrots and potato. Lower heat and simmer until vegetables are very tender. Puree in blender in small batches. Return to heat.

Cha Cha's White Chicken Chili
Cindy Totty

1 Tbsp. vegetable oil
1 onion, chopped
3 cloves garlic, crushed
1 (4 oz.) can jalapeno peppers
1 (4 oz.) can chopped green chiles
2 tsp. ground cumin
1 cup shredded Monterey jack cheese
1 tsp. dried oregano
1 tsp. ground cayenne pepper
2 (14.5 oz.) cans chicken broth
3 cups chopped chicken breast
3 (15 oz.) cans white beans

Heat the oil in a large saucepan over medium-low heat. Slowly cook and stir the onion until tender. Mix in the garlic, jalapeno, green chiles peppers, cumin, oregano and cayenne. Continue to cook and stir the mixture until tender, about 3 minutes. Mix in the chicken broth, chicken and white beans. Simmer 15 minutes, stirring occasionally. Remove the mixture from heat. Slowly stir in the cheese until melted. Serve warm.

Chicken Caesar Salad
Banks Corl

Rotisserie Chicken
1/2 cup Cardini's Original Caesar dressing, or similar
6 cups hand shredded Romaine lettuce
2 cups garlic croutons
1/2 cup pre-shredded Parmesan cheese

Wash, separate, and lay out the Romaine on paper towels. Hand shred to a fairly fine consistency (fork ready) into a large mixing or salad bowl. Then filet out both chicken breasts from the roasted chicken and remove the skin. You can find some additional white meat next to the wings underneath if you need more. Cut the chicken into bite sized pieces or longer strips. Mix in the dressing, cheese, and chicken. If serving right away, mix in the garlic croutons. If not, then add them at the last minute so they don't get soggy.

Chemo Chicken Soup
Keith and Lee Ann Martin

This soup is great if you know someone who is going through chemotherapy. It definitely helps with the 'metal' aftertaste of chemo, and the nausea. It is one of those things that is easy to eat, even when you don't feel like eating!

1 medium onion, chopped
3 ribs celery, thinly sliced
2 Tbsp. margarine
1 can (14 ½ oz.) chicken broth
4 chicken bouillon cubes, dissolved in 4 cups boiling water
½ cup carrot matchsticks or thin slices
2 very large baking potatoes, peeled and cubed
1 tsp. salt
¼ tsp. black pepper
1 Tbsp. dried parsley
20 oz. prepared refrigerated mashed potatoes

Sauté onion and celery in margarine. Add liquid, carrots, cubed potatoes and seasoning. Simmer until potatoes are soft. Stir in prepared mashed potatoes and bring to a boil while stirring.

Chicken Salad
Marilyn Downer

1 cup chopped pecans
1/2 cup mayonnaise
1/4 cup sweet minced onion
2 Tbsp. basil
1/2 tsp. salt & pepper
4 small peaches, diced
4 cups cooked chicken, chopped

Garnish: Blackberries

Combine ingredients except basil and blackberries. Garnish. Chill. Serve on lettuce leaves.

Chicken and Rice Soup
Terry Richards

4 boneless chicken breast
3 Tbsp. butter
6 Wyler's Chicken Bullion
Uncle Ben's ready rice, wild and long grain
1 can (32 oz.) Swanson chicken broth
Small can diced carrots
Morton Nature's Seasoning, garlic, oregano, pepper, minced onions (to taste)

Put chicken breasts into a crock pot with 1/2 cup of water and 3 bullion cubes. Season to taste. I put Morton Natures Seasoning, garlic, oregano, very little salt (the bullion cubes are salty), pepper, minced onion. 1 Tbsp butter and let cook for 1 1/2 hours. When the chicken is tender remove form crock pot and cut into small pieces and put chicken back into crock pot. Add the chicken broth and 2 more Tbsp of butter. Let cook on high until broth is hot. Add a small can of sliced carrots (drained). Microwave the rice for 90 seconds, as directed on package; add rice to soup. Stir and serve. ENJOY!!!

Chicken Vegetable Soup
Megan Johnson

1 can chicken
1/2 onion
1 Tbsp. cornstarch
1 large can chicken broth
3 stalks celery- sautéed
1 package noodles
5 Tbsp. chicken flavor soup base in cold water

Mix all ingredients except noodles and cook for 1-2 hours. Cook noodles and drain. Add noodles to soup mixture and let simmer 30 min- 1 hour.

Chicken Noodle Soup
Julia Baron

4 48 oz. can chicken broth
5 stalks celery, chopped
5 carrots, peeled and chopped
1 med. onion, chopped
1/4 cup finely chopped fresh dill
1/4 cup finely chopped fresh parsley
1 Rotisserie chicken, de-boned and cut into pieces
1/2 stick butter
1/2 tsp. salt
1/2 tsp. white pepper
3-4 cloves garlic, chopped
1 tsp. Nature's Seasons Seasoning Blend
1 bag egg noodles

Sauté onion, celery and garlic in butter in a large stock pot. When onion is soft, add carrots. Cook 2 minutes on medium heat, add broth and rest of ingredients, except noodles. Bring to boil 2-3 minutes, drop heat to low and cook 1 hour. Then add noodles, bring to boil again, boil 2 minutes, drop heat to low and cook 2 more hours. Salt and pepper to taste. ENJOY!!

Clam Chowder
Tim Passmore

2 large cans of clams
10 strips of bacon
8 small red potatoes
2 cups of whole milk
Salt and pepper
1 cup of clam juice
1 large sweet onion
2 cup of cream
4 Tbsp. of butter
Hot sauce

Cut up potatoes in to cubes. Cook the potatoes in the clam juice until fork tender. Cook the bacon and set aside. Chop the onions and sauté them in a large soup pot until they are golden brown. Add the cream, milk and the potatoes with the juice. Add the two cans of clams, salt, pepper and some hot sauce. Crumble the bacon in and allow to simmer for an hour.

Clam Chowder
Rae Sprow

1/2 pound bacon, diced	1 cup finely chopped onion
1 cup chopped celery	1 cup chopped carrots, peeled
1 quart chicken stock	Salt
Freshly ground black pepper	3 bay leaves
1/2 cup flour	1 Tbsp. chopped fresh thyme
4 cups clam juice	1 pkg. frozen hash brown potatoes
2 cups Half-and-Half	3/4 cup butter, melted

3/4 cup all-purpose flour 4 cans minced clams with liquid
Dry sherry to taste (approx. 1 cup)

In a heavy stock pot, cook bacon until crisp. Drain, reserving 2 tablespoons drippings in pan. Crumble bacon and set aside. Stir in the onions, celery, and carrots. Sauté for about 2 minutes or until the vegetables start to wilt. Season the vegetables with salt and pepper. Add the bay leaves and thyme. Stir in the flour and cook for 2 minutes. Add the potatoes. Stir in the clam juice. Bring the liquid up to a boil and reduce to a simmer until potatoes are soft, 2o minutes. Stir in Half-and-Half. Combine melted butter and flour, then whisk into soup. Cook and stir until thickened. Stir in clams with liquid and dry sherry. Remove bay leaves. Stir in bacon. Yields: 8 servings

Cranberry Orange Jello Mold
Gloria Kurlinski

2 10-oz. cans mandarin oranges	3/4 cup boiling water
2 cans whole cranberry sauce, drained	1 6-oz. pkg. of cherry jello
1 cup sour cream	

Drain oranges, reserve syrup. Combine jello and water, stir until clear. Add cranberries, reserved syrup, and mix. Chill until egg white consistency. Beat until fluffy. Fold in oranges and sour cream. Spoon into a jello mold and chill until set. Remove from mold and serve with walnut garnish, if desired. Or fold walnuts in jello mixture before chilling.

Chicken Tortilla Soup
Betsy Hall

2 Tbsp. olive oil
1 1/2 cups onion, chopped
2 Tbsp. garlic, minced
3 corn tortilla (6"), cut in 1" pieces (crispy or regular)
1 can diced tomatoes/green chiles (Rotel tomatoes)
4 cups chicken broth (low sodium/fat free)
1 tsp. ground cumin
1 tsp. ground coriander
1/2 tsp. cayenne pepper
1 tsp. dried oregano
2 cups cooked turkey or chicken (I use Sam's Rotisserie chicken)
1 1/2 cups garbanzos, drained (or can corned, drained)
1 cup of cooked carrots, diced in bite size pieces (optional)
1/2 cup heavy cream (I use the low calorie one)
1 cup Monterey jack cheese, shredded
2 Tbsp. fresh lime (or less)

Heat olive oil in large soup pot. Add onions and garlic and sauté 3 min. Stir in tortilla pieces and sauté until no longer crisp (add soft ones with tomatoes, etc.) Add tomatoes, broth, spices and bring to boil. Remove from heat. Cool 5 mins or longer. Then puree soup base in blender in 1 cup intervals (soup is still very hot...do not rush this part, small amts at a time)...pouring the "puree" out into a soup pot after each blending. Add chicken or turkey, garbanzos beans (or corn), carrots, cream. Bring to a boil and simmer about 5 min. until starts to thicken. Reduce heat to medium. Sprinkle cheese and stir until melted. Add fresh squeezed lime and season with salt and pepper (to taste). I always double this recipe...I figure if I am going to work this hard to make this...I might as well share a batch or freeze a batch!

Cool Cucumber Soup
Jannon Pierce

3 chopped cucumbers
1 cup sour cream
1 cup plain yogurt
1 minced garlic clove
2 Tbsp. chopped parsley
2 cups chicken stock
1 tsp. salt
1/2 tsp. pepper
Chives

Puree cucumbers, sour cream, yogurt, garlic and parsley. Add chicken stock, salt and pepper to taste. Chill and garnish with sliced chives, paprika and a dollop of sour cream.

Creamy Italian Pasta Salad
Rae Sprow

1 lb. Rotini/Rotelle Pasta, cooked, rinsed in cold water and drained
2 cups cubed cheddar cheese
2-3 stalks celery, finely chopped
1 lb. cooked Italian sausage or Kielbasa, cut into bite size pieces
1 each green, yellow & red bell pepper, diced
1 cup black olives, slivered
2 cups cherry tomatoes, quartered
1/4 cup chopped fresh basil

Dressing:
1 pint mayonnaise
2 tsp. salt
2-3 cloves garlic, finely minced
1/4 cup red wine vinegar
2 Tbsp. dried basil leaves
1/2 tsp. black or white pepper

Combine dressing ingredients in large bowl. Stir in pasta, cheese, tomatoes, Kielbasa, peppers, celery, basil and olives. Cover and chill.

Craisin Salad
Andreah Wellman

1 head red lettuce
1 head iceberg lettuce
1 head green leaf lettuce
8 oz. shredded mozzarella cheese
6 oz. shredded parmesan cheese
1 cup Craisins (dried cranberries)
1/2 cup green onions-chopped very fine
1 lb. bacon (can use turkey bacon)
4-6 boneless/skinless chicken breasts, cooked and cubed
1/2 cup toasted, sliced almonds (cooled)
DRESSING: Mix in blender: 1 cup white sugar,
2 tsp. dry mustard,
1/2 cup red wine vinegar (good quality),
1 cup canola oil (do not substitute)

Wash lettuces, dry well. Tear into bite sized pieces. Put lettuces in largest bowl you have. Sprinkle on cheeses and onion and mix lightly. Cook bacon and crumble. Add Craisins, almonds, bacon and chicken just before serving. (For added taste, BBQ chicken can be used) Before serving, pour dressing (as desired) on salad and mix well. The dressing makes the salad. The salad can be made the day before. Store in the refrigerator, in an airtight container. Do not pour dressing on until ready to serve. Makes a very large salad. Enjoy!

Dave O's Calico Beans
Bonnie Swete

1 lb. hamburger meat
1/2 cup onion, chopped
1/2 lb. of bacon, browned and crumbled
1 21-oz. can of pork & beans
1 medium can of butter beans or lima beans
1 medium can of kidney beans
Drain the butter beans and kidney beans and reserve 1/3 cup of liquid from each

1/2 cup of catsup
1/2 cup of packed brown sugar
1 Tbsp. vinegar
1 Tbsp. mustard

Brown the hamburger meat and onions in a deep pan. Drain excess oil. Add all the remaining ingredients along with the hamburger meat and onions back to the pan. Allow to simmer until warm. It is ready to serve. Recipe makes approx. 8 servings. *Be creative! Other meat like sausage is good as well. Or try mushrooms!

Heavenly Salad
Kim Barger

1 cup cubed canned pineapple, drained well
1 cup mandarin oranges, drained well
1 cup red grapes, sliced in half
1 cup small marshmallows
1 cup coconut
3/4 cup sour cream

Mix all the ingredients except sour cream. Then add sour cream and chill.

Easy Elegant Mandarin Salad
Marge Wise

1/2 head iceberg or romaine lettuce
1 cup chopped celery
1 large can mandarin oranges, drained
1 Tbsp. butter
4 Tbsp. sugar
1/2 cup slivered almonds
2 Tbsp. cider vinegar
1/2 cup oil
1/4 tsp. salt
1 tsp. parsley
Few drops of Tabasco sauce

Gently toss lettuce, celery, and oranges. Brown together butter, 2 Tbsp sugar, and almonds. Watch closely so they do not burn. Turn out onto tin foil to cool then sprinkle over lettuce mix. Mix together well remaining sugar and all remaining ingredients. Pour over salad just before serving.

Gazpacho
Patty Phillips

1 cucumber, peeled and chopped
1 small onion, diced
1/2 green pepper, diced
2 small tomatoes, peeled and chopped
1/2 avocado, peeled and chopped
4 cups tomato juice (or V-8)
3 Tbsp. olive oil
2 Tbsp. red wine vinegar
1/2 tsp. oregano

Mix all and chill at least 2 hours. Serve with a dollop of sour cream and a dash of celery salt. You can also add croutons. Great to make ahead of your guest arriving. Also great in the summer time. Enjoy****

Curried Cauliflower Soup
Pam Herrington

2 tsp. oil 1 large onion, chopped
2 medium carrots, sliced 1/4 inch thick
2 Tbsp. curry powder
2 cloves garlic, minced
2 cans (14.5 oz. each) chicken broth, or 3 1/2 cups broth or boullion
2 1/2 cups water
2 medium potatoes, cut into 1/2 in pieces
3 cups frozen cauliflower florets
1 can (15.5 oz.) chickpeas, rinsed
1/2 cup frozen cut-leaf spinach
Serve with: plain yogurt

Heat oil in large saucepan over medium-high heat. Add onions and carrots; cook 4 minutes or until onions are golden and just tender. Stir in curry powder and garlic; cook 30 seconds or until fragrant. Stir in remaining ingredients; cook, covered, 15 minutes or until vegetables are tender.

Ginger Cucumber Salad
Pam Herrington

2 Tbsp. pre-sliced green onions
2 Tbsp. pickled ginger (sushi gari)
1/4 cup refrigerated
Oriental salad dressing
1/4 cup rice vinegar
1/4 tsp. pepper
2 medium cucumbers (rinsed)

Place all ingredients (except cucumbers) in large bowl. Peel cucumber; cut into ribbons. To do this lay each cucumber flat on work surface. Cut thin slices, using a vegetable peeler, down the entire length of cucumber until reaching the seeds. Turn cucumber and continue cutting ribbons on each side, avoiding the seeds until only the seeds remain. Add ribbons to bowl (about 1 1/2 cups); discard seeds. Toss evenly until coated; chill until ready to serve

Italian Sausage and Tortellini Soup
Andreah Wellman

1 lb. sweet Italian sausage
1 cup chopped onion
2 large garlic cloves, chopped
5 cups beef stock
28 oz. can plum tomatoes
18 oz. can tomato sauce
1 large zucchini, chopped
2 carrots, thinly sliced
1 medium green pepper, diced
1/2 cup dry red wine
2 Tbsp. basil
2 Tbsp. oregano
8 or 10 oz. package of fresh cheese tortellini fresh
Grated parmesan cheese for top before serving

Sauté 1 pound sweet Italian sausage, breaking up with spoon. Drain sausage, reserving 1 tablespoon drippings, remove sausage to bowl to reserved fat, add onion and garlic, sauté until onion is transparent. Add sausage back to pot, add all remaining ingredients except parmesan cheese and tortellini's. Simmer 45 minutes or until vegetables are tender. Add tortellini's, and simmer 8-10 minutes more. Serve with freshly grated parmesan cheese over soup, and crusty bread. Delicious. Enjoy!!

Layered Salad
Angela Dyches

1 head of lettuce washed in salt water, drained and chopped
1 bell pepper, chopped
3 boiled eggs, chopped
1 sm. pkg. of frozen peas, cooked and cooled
1 sm. red onion, chopped
1/2 pkg. of bacon, cooked and crumbled
1 pt of Hellman's mayonnaise (only use Hellman's)
1/4 c sugar
2 cups cheddar cheese, shredded

Mix 1 pt of Hellman's mayonnaise and 1/4 c of sugar together in a separate bowl. Layer first 6 items and top with the mayo/sugar mixture. Sprinkle cheese over mayo/sugar mixture. Chill in the refrigerator. Best if made the day before. Serves 8.

Mama's Super Sonic Chili
Holly McAndrew

2 cans chili beans
1 can condensed tomato soup
Chili powder
1/2 lb. hamburger
1 cup chopped onion (optional)

In a large microwaveable bowl, cook hamburger (and onion) in microwave for 6 minutes, breaking up and draining hamburger after 3 minutes. If, necessary, continue cooking in 2 minute increments until brown. Add chili beans & tomato soup. Fill each chili bean can 1/4 full of water and add to bowl. Mix together. Season to taste with chili powder. Cover and heat in microwave for 3 minutes or until heated through.

Meg's White Chicken Chili
Megan Lynn

1 Tbsp. olive oil or vegetable oil
1 med onion, chopped (1/2 cup)
1/2 cup red bell pepper, chopped
1 can condensed cream of chicken soup
1 can chicken broth
1 cup water
2 cups diced cooked, chicken
2 cans great northern beans, drained and rinsed
1/2 tsp. Ground Cumin   1/2 tsp. Dried Oregano

In 4-quart saucepan, heat oil over med-high heat. Add onions & bell pepper. Cook 2-3 min. Stir in soup, broth and water. Cook 1-2 min. Stir until smooth. Stir chicken, beans, oregano & cumin. Heat to boiling, reduce heat to med-low. Cook uncovered 10-15 min. Stir occasionally, until thoroughly heated. 6 servings

Orange Salad
Carol Williams

1 pkg. orange jello   1 cup nuts (chopped)
1 cup boiling water   1 can Mandarin oranges
½ cup sugar   1/2 pint sour cream
1 small can crushed pineapple

Mix jello, sugar and water until dissolved. Add other ingredients and mold.

Navy Bean Soup – Vegan
Erlida Waters

2 Tbsp. olive oil
2 garlic, medium, minced
1 cup onions, chopped
5 cups waters
2 cups potatoes, 1/2" cubed
1 3/4 tsp. sea salt
2 cups frozen chopped kale (partially thawed)
1/4 tsp. cumin
2 Tbsp. nutritional yeast flakes (available at health food stores)
3 cups navy beans, cooked
1/3 cup Vegenaise (to give creamy effect) (available at health food stores)

In pot, briefly sauté garlic in olive oil. Add onions and continue to sauté until clear. Put in next six ingredients. Cover and cook over medium-high heat until potatoes are done (about 20 minutes). Add beans and Vegenaise. Cook for several more minutes and serve. If using salt free beans, use 2 1/2 tsp salt instead of 1 3/4 tsp. Can add 2 Tbsp Vegenaise. Yield: 8 cups

Red Wine Vinaigrette Salad
Marge Wise

1 bag spring mix (I also add romaine and baby spinach)
Crumbled gorgonzola cheese
Toasted pine nuts

Dressing:
3 Tbsp. canola oil
2 Tbsp. red wine vinega
1/4 tsp. pepper
1 clove garlic
3 Tbsp. olive oil
1/4 tsp. salt
1/4 tsp. sugar

Mix well, makes about 1/2 cup. Pour dressing on greens just before serving...enjoy!

Pasta Fagioli Soup
Reba Pearson

1 lb. ground Beef
1 small onion, diced (1 cup)
1 large carrot, julienned (1 cup)
3 stalks celery, chopped (1 cup)
2 cloves garlic, minced
2 14.5-oz. cans diced tomatoes
1 15-oz. can red kidney beans, with liquid
1 15-oz. can northern beans, with liquid
1 15-oz. can tomato sauce
1 12-oz. can V-8 juice
1 Tbsp. white vinegar
1 1/2 tsp. salt
1 tsp. oregano
1 tsp. basil
1/2 tsp. pepper
1/2 tsp. thyme
1/2 lb. (1/2 pkg.) Ditalia Pasta

Brown the ground beef in a large saucepan or pot over medium heat, Drain off most of the fat .Add onions, carrot, celery, and garlic and sauté for 10 minutes. Add remaining ingredients, except pasta, and simmer for 1 hour. About 50 minutes into simmer time, cook for 10 minutes or just until pasta is al dente (or slightly tough) and drain. Add the pasta to the large pot of soup. Simmer for 5-10 minutes and serve.

Potato-Bacon-and-Leek Soup
Judy Daniels

4 thick cut slices of bacon
4 leeks thinly sliced
3 14 oz. cans chicken broth
3 lbs Yukon gold potatoes, peeled and cut into 3/4 in. cubes
8 oz. Gruyere cheese, shredded
3/4 tsp. salt
1/2 tsp. pepper
2 Tbsp. chopped parsley

Cook bacon in a large pot over med.-high heat until crisp, remove and set aside. Spoon off all but 1 Tbsp of the dripping. Place leeks in pot and cook, stirring often, until tender, (about 7 min.) Add broth and potatoes and bring to a boil. Cover and cook until potatoes are tender, (about 10 min.) Remove 2 cups of the potatoes with a slotted spoon and place in a food processor along with the Gruyere cheese, puree until mixture is smooth. Stirring constantly until cheese is melted (2min). Do not allow soup to boil. Crumble bacon and stir into soup along with salt and pepper, and parsley. Makes 10 cups.

Spinach Salad
Lynn Francisco

1 lb. spinach
2 chopped eggs
6 slices of bacon croutons

Dressing:
2 tsp. vinegar
1/2 cup milk
1/3 cup mayonnaise
1/4 or 1/2 cup sugar

Mix all ingredients and pour dressing (shake well) on when ready to serve.

Quick Chili Con Carne
Bonnie Swete

1 lb. ground beef
1 cup of chopped onion (or more)
1/2 cup of water
2 cans (1 lb. each) of kidney beans, undrained
1 can of condensed tomato soup
1 Tbsp. of oil
1 tsp. of vinegar
2 cloves of minced garlic
2 to 3 tsp. chili powder
1/2 tsp. of salt
Dash of pepper

Cook beef, onion, garlic and seasonings in oil until the meat is lightly browned. Add remaining ingredients. Cover and cook over low heat for 30 minutes; stir often. Uncover and cook to desired consistency. Makes enough for 4 servings.

Taco Soup
Samantha Slade

1 lrg. onion, chopped
1 pkg. taco seasoning
2 cups frozen whole kernel corn
1 can great northern beans, undrained
1 can diced tomatoes with jalapenos
1 lb. ground beef
1 can fat free chicken broth
1 can black beans, undrained
1 can fat free refried beans
1 can diced tomatoes

In a large pot, sauté the onion with the ground beef until done. Add all other ingredients and simmer for 30-40 minutes stirring occasionally. Serve hot.

Quick & Easy Low Fat Tex-Mex Chili
Georgie Mygrant

1 1/2 lb. of turkey breast
1 small can of corn
2 tsp. of chili powder
1 cup of cooked macaroni
2 cans of beans with chili sauce
1 small onion, chopped
Tomato juice

Hot peppers, or hot sauce if desired, but can be left out and it will still be good.

Brown turkey with onions. Add beans with sauce, corn, chili powder, and macaroni. Mix well. Add tomato juice to make a good soup consistency. (More if you like it runny, or less if you like it thick!) Cook, covered, over low heat for 30 minutes. Serve in large bowls, with oyster crackers. Sprinkle light shredded cheese over top and a dab of fat-free sour cream. If you like it hot, you can add hot sauce, or hot peppers during cooking! This recipe can be made with light fat ground beef as well, but it won't be as fat free as with turkey. Either way, it's great! You can double, triple, or more, for a large group of people. I usually serve over 50 people on New Years day with this recipe. They all love it and keep coming back for more! Enjoy!

Wilted Spinach Salad
Sharon Schroeter

1/2 bag [5oz.] fresh baby spinach
1/4 cup toasted sliced almonds
1/4 cup real bacon bits
1/4 cup sugar
1/4 cup vinegar
1/4 cup dried cranberries
2 tsp. dried minced onion

Put spinach & almonds in large bowl. Heat bacon bits 2-3 minutes. Add sugar, vinegar, cranberries & onion and cook 2-3 minutes. Pour over spinach & almonds & mix together.

Salad with Fruit and Poppy Seed Dressing
Sue Powell

Salad:
Romaine lettuce torn cut up
Apples, strawberries, grapes, blueberries and canned mandarin oranges
Sliced red onion
Candied nuts
Crumbled blue cheese (optional)

Poppy Seed Dressing:

1/3 cup honey	2 Tbsp. vinegar
1 Tbsp. lemon juice	1/2 tsp. salt
1 tsp. dry mustard	1 Tbsp. grated onion
3/4 cup olive oil	1 Tbsp. poppy seed

Dressing: Combine vinegar and honey in blender or with whisk. Add lemon juice, salt, dry mustard and onion. Slowly add oil. When blended, add poppy seed and chill.

Strawberry Salad
Marge Wise

1 head romaine lettuce (I often make this half baby spinach)
1 pint slivered strawberries
1/2 sweet onion, sliced thinly

Dressing:
(I double and triple this recipe because keeps well if refrigerated)
1/2 cup mayonnaise (I use light mayo)
2 Tbsp. raspberry vinegar (not balsamic)
1/3 cup sugar (I use Splenda)
1/8 cup skim or whole milk
1/2 tsp. poppy seeds

Layer lettuce, then strawberries and onions. Mix dressing in jar. Shake well. Pour over salad just before serving. I have also made this with spinach, apples, walnuts, blue cheese, and sweet onions.

Taco Salad
Wilhelmina Ellerments

1 lb. ground beef
1 small onion, diced
1 pkg. taco seasoning mix
2 large tomatoes, chopped
2 cups cheddar cheese, shredded
1 12-16 oz. bag taco flavored chips, crushed
16 oz. French dressing
1/4 cup taco sauce

Brown hamburger and onion in skillet. Add taco seasoning mix. Set aside to cool. Toss chopped lettuce with tomatoes and cheese. Add beef mixture and taco chips. Combine French dressing and taco sauce. Add to lettuce mixture and toss gently. The ingredients of this salad may be prepared ahead of time but do not combine them longer than 15-30 minutes before serving. ENJOY!

Strawberry Pretzel Salad
Brian and Betsy Hall and girls

STEP ONE- 1 cup pretzels, crushed
3 Tbsp sugar
1/2 cup of melted margarine

Mix together and pat into a 9x13 pan. Bake at 350 for 10 minutes. Cool.

STEP TWO- 1 8 oz cream cheese, softened
1 scant cup sugar
1 small container of Cool Whip

Mix together and pour on cooled crust. Refrigerate until firm.

STEP THREE- 1 6 oz package of strawberry jello
2 cups boiling water
1 large package frozen strawberries with sugar

Mix together, refrigerate, and when it starts to jell, spoon over the cheese layer. Refrigerate overnight or until completely jelled.

PLEASE NOTE:
Do not use the stick pretzels as they will crush too fine. I use the light cream cheese and the light cool whip. I cannot find a 16 oz package of frozen strawberries, so I use two 10 oz packages. I measure out two cups and it works fine. This is a Thanksgiving and Christmas favorite at our house and one of Molly's favorites!

White Chicken Chili
Maria Biegel

1/4 cup butter
1 large onion, chopped (1 cup)
1 garlic clove, chopped
4 cups of chicken, 1/2 in. cubed/cooked (can use turkey)
3 cups of chicken broth
2 Tbsp. chopped fresh cilantro
1 Tbsp. dried basil leaves
1/4 tsp. chili powder
1/4 tsp. ground cloves
2 cans of great northern beans, undrained
Blue tortilla chips
Shredded cheese
Sour cream

Melt butter in 4 quart Dutch-oven over medium heat. Cook onion and garlic in butter, stirring occasionally until onion is tender. Stir in remaining ingredients. (not chips, cheese, sour cream) Heat to boil, reduce heat. Cover and let simmer 1 hour, stirring occasionally. Serve with tomato, tortilla chips, cheese, and sour cream.

White Chicken Chili
Shea Haupt

1 lrg. onion
1 tsp. garlic powder
1 tsp. oil
2 cans great northern beans (not drained)
3 cups diced cooked chicken
1 (14.5 oz.) can chicken broth
2 tsp. cumin
2 tsp. chili powder
1/2 tsp. oregano
1/4 tsp. cayenne pepper

Sauté onions in oil until tender. Add remaining ingredients and simmer 30 minutes. Garnish with sour cream, shredded cheese, green onions, or cilantro and serve with chips

Entrees

So I tell you, don't worry about everyday life--whether you have enough food, drink, and clothes. Doesn't life consist of more than food and clothing? Look at the birds. They don't need to plant or harvest or put food in barns because your heavenly Father feeds them. And you are far more valuable to him than they are."
Matthew 6:25-26

Entrees

Alfredo Sauce
Jennifer Passmore

2 cups heavy cream
4 oz. cream cheese
1 glove garlic
1 stick of butter
1 cup Parmesan cheese
Salt and pepper

Sauté garlic in two tablespoons of the butter. Do not over cook the garlic because it will turn bitter. Add the remaining butter and cream cheese, turn temperature down to low and melt butter and cream cheese. Add heavy cream and cook on low for 15 minutes. Stir often. Add parmesan cheese and bring heat up to medium for 5 minutes stirring constantly. Serve over fettuccine.

Apricot Chicken
Licia White

4 boneless (skinless) chicken breast
1/2 jar of apricot jam
1 bottle of Catalina or French dressing
1 envelope of Lipton onion soup mix

Line casserole dish with foil and place chicken on top. Mix together all other ingredients and pour mixture over chicken. Bake at 375 for 40 min. (until chicken is done). Suggested: Serve with rice or baked potatoes.

Baked Fish
Jean McIntyre

2 1/4 – 3 1/2 lb. of any fish fillet   1cup crushed Ritz crackers
1 cup Panko crispy bread crumbs   1/4 cup mayonnaise (Real)
1/3 cup of Polaner All Fruit Seedless Raspberry

Preheat oven to 350. Spray cookie sheet with Pam. Rinse fish and pat dry. With butter knife spread mayonnaise over fish very lightly. Then roll fish in mixer of crushed Ritz & Panko Crumbs, cover completely. After all fillets are on cookie sheet take remaining crumbs and put on top of fillets. Bake 10 -15 minutes (depending on size of fillets) until fish is done (meat will be white and flaky). Do Not Over Bake. To kick your fish up an extra notch, try this! Take Polaner All Fruit Seedless Raspberry Spread and micro-wave for 20 second until liquid, just before serving fish drizzle lightly over fish. YUM!

"Barbie" cups
Betsy Hall

1 lb. ground beef or turkey
1/2 cup prepared barbecue sauce (sweet ones are the best)
1/4 cup chopped onions
1-2 Tbsp. brown sugar (unless using a sweet bbq sauce)
1 (10 oz.) can Hungry Jack Refrigerated flaky biscuits
2 oz. (1/2 cup) low fat cheddar cheese (shredded)

Heat oven to 400. Grease 10 muffin cups (can make 12 or a sheet of mini's - break each roll in two if you do mini's). Brown in a large skillet and drain grease. Stir in bbq sauce, onion, and brown sugar. Cook 1 minute to blend flavors, stirring constantly. Separate dough into 10 biscuits (the meat is enough to make 12). Place one biscuit in each tin and spread out. Firmly press bottom and up sides of each muffin tin. Making a small border around the top of each, spoon meat to the top of each tin. Sprinkle with cheese. Bake for 10-12 minutes (keep watch) or until edges are golden brown. SERVINGS: 10. My mom's (Barbara James) favorite recipe that became my girls favorite. We miss you! GAP...God Always Provides!!

Barbecued Shrimp
Shea Haupt

3 lbs gulf shrimp in shells
2 cloves garlic, chopped
1/2 tsp. onion salt
Juice of 1 lemon
1/2 tsp. red pepper
2 sticks butter
1/2 tsp. garlic salt
1 1/2 tsp. black pepper
1 Tbsp. Worcestershire sauce

Melt butter in large shallow pan (Dutch-oven works great). Add garlic, pepper, lemon juice and Worcestershire sauce. Brown slightly. Add shrimp. Sprinkle with garlic and onion salts. Bake at 350 for about 30 minutes, depending on size of shrimp. Stir once. Serve with French bread or crusty rolls.

Basic Stir-fry Blackened Chicken
Pam Patterson

4 chicken breast, cut in strips
Blackened seasoning
1 bag stir-fry veggies
1-2 Tbsp. butter

Chicken breast into strips. Season the chicken with the blackened seasoning. Put butter in pan and heat until melted. Add chicken strips. Sauté over medium heat until done. Add vegetables. Cook until tender. Serve.

"Bertke" Meat Loaf
Bruce and Hilary Bertke

2 lbs ground beef
1/2 cup green pepper, chopped
1/4 cup bread crumbs

1/4 tsp. nutmeg
Salt and pepper
2 Tbsp. Worcestershire sauce

1/2 cup onion, chopped
1/4 cup celery, chopped
1 Tbsp. chopped basil and parsley

3 Tbsp. Maggi sauce
1 egg

Mix all ingredients together. Pack well in loaf pan.

GLAZE
1 cup brown sugar
1/4 cup beer

2 tsp. dry mustard

Mix together. Baste meatloaf while cooking with glaze
Bake at 375 for 1 1/2 hours.

Broiled Catfish with Bread Crumbs
Pam Herrington

4 catfish fillets (6-8 oz.)
1/2 tsp. salt
1 Tbsp. minced garlic
1 tsp. fresh thyme leaves
2 tsp. Emerils Essence or Creole seasoning

1/4 cup fresh bread crumbs
1/4 tsp. white pepper
4 Tbsp. extra virgin olive oil
1 lemon - juiced

Preheat oven to broil setting - rack 6" from broiler unit. Season catfish on both sides with Essence, salt and white pepper. Place on an aluminum foil lined baking sheet. In small bowl combine garlic, 2 Tbsp olive oil and thyme - stir to blend. Use small spoon to dab mixture evenly over fish. Drizzle lemon juice over fish and sprinkle with 1 Tbsp of bread crumbs. Drizzle remaining olive oil over bread crumbs. Place fish under broiler to cook 6-7 min. Turn around and cook another 6-7 min or until the crumbs are golden brown. Remove and serve immediately.

Brown Sugar and Soy Sauce Salmon
Pam Herrington

1/4 cup soy sauce
1/4 tsp. crushed red pepper
1/8 tsp. sesame oil
2 Tbsp. brown sugar
1/4 tsp. ground ginger
Fillet of salmon

Mix all ingredients together and marinade salmon. Wrap in foil and bake on grill or in oven (350 degrees) 5-6 minutes on each side while basting frequently.

Brown-Sugar-Glazed Salmon
Rae Sprow

1/4 cup packed dark-brown sugar
2 tsp. Dijon mustard
8 oz. steamed snow peas
2 tsp. butter, melted
1/4 tsp. each salt and pepper
2 cups cooked brown rice
4 2-inch wide salmon fillets (about 1 1/2 pounds total)

Preheat oven to 325. Line a small baking sheet with nonstick aluminum foil. Place salmon on prepared sheet. In a small bowl, stir together brown sugar, butter, mustard, salt and pepper. Carefully spread over salmon pieces, dividing equally. Transfer salmon to oven and bake for 25 minutes, or until fish flakes easily with a fork. Serve with snow peas and rice on side.

Bubble Up Pizza
Joy Coblentz

2 pkg. Grande biscuits
1 lb. shredded mozzarella
1 large jar spaghetti sauce
Toppings to taste

Preheat oven to 375. Spray a 9x13 pan. Cut biscuits into 1/8 pieces. Put 1/2 sauce in the bottom of pan. Put in biscuits. Layer on toppings. Spread rest of sauce on. Sprinkle with mozzarella. Bake 25-30 minute or until golden brown.

Cajun Chicken Pasta
Durst Family

Chicken breast chunks
1/2 tsp. pepper
/4 tsp. salt
1/4 tsp. lemon pepper
4 oz. Linguine - cooked
2 Tbsp. butter
1/4 tsp. dried basil
2 cups heavy cream
1/8 tsp. garlic
Parmesan cheese
2 tsp. Cajun Seas (*Durkee Grill Creations Cajun seasoning)

Toss chicken in Cajun Seas seasoning. Sauté in butter 5-7 minutes or until done. Reduce heat. Add cream & seasonings. Stir. Toss with linguine. Serve with Parmesan cheese.

Cheesy Chicken Spaghetti
Tina Yoder

1 cut up chicken
1 can cream of mushroom soup
1 stick of butter
1 cup of small diced bell pepper
1 large package of thin spaghetti
1 large jar Cheese Whiz
1 can cream of celery soup
1 cup diced onion

Boil chicken until tender. Drain broth into a pot and reserve to cook the spaghetti in. Cut up the chicken into bite-size pieces and set aside. Cook the onion and bell pepper in the butter on the stove until the onions are clear and peppers tender. Break up the dry spaghetti, and then cook in the broth per package instruction while the onions are cooking. Add the Cheese Whiz and soups to the onions and simmer until warm and the cheese is melted and mixed well. Remove spaghetti, drain and put back in a large pot. Add the diced chicken and cheese/onion sauce to the spaghetti and mix well. Season to taste with salt and pepper. Turn into 2 buttered casserole dishes (one for you and one for a neighbor). Bake uncovered at 350 for 30-40 minutes.

Cheese Enchiladas
Claudia Mathis

25 corn tortillas
5 green chile peppers
4 carrots, diced
1 onion, finely chopped
1 head of lettuce, chopped
1 pound cheese, grated
5 large potatoes, diced
5 jalapeno peppers
1 cup vegetable oil

Boil the green chile peppers and puree the water and chile mixture. Salt to taste. Combine the cheese and onion. Heat the oil in a skillet. Dip each tortilla in the chile salsa and fry. Add cheese mixture to each fried tortilla and roll. In a separate pan, fry the potatoes and carrots and also add some of the chile salsa. Serve the enchiladas (rolled tortillas) with the potatoes and carrots on the side. Also add the chopped lettuce as a side dish.

Chicago-Style Pan Pizza
Andrea V. Johnston

1 refrigerated rolled pizza dough
1/2 lb. sliced fresh mushrooms
2 tsp. olive oil
1 can (28 oz.) diced tomatoes, drained
1/2 tsp. fennel seed, crushed
1 lb. Italian sausage roll
1 small onion, chopped
3/4 tsp. dried oregano
1/2 tsp. salt
1/4 tsp. garlic powder
2 cups (8 oz.) shredded part-skim mozzarella cheese
1/2 cup grated parmesan cheese

Press dough onto the bottom and up the sides of a greased 13 x 9 in. baking dish. In a large skillet, cook sausage over medium heat until no longer pink; drain. Sprinkle over dough. Top with mozzarella cheese. In a skillet, sauté mushrooms and onion in oil until onion is tender. Stir in the tomatoes, oregano, salt, fennel seed and garlic powder. Spoon over mozzarella cheese. Sprinkle with parmesan cheese. Bake at 350 for 25-35 min. or until crust is golden brown.

Chicken and Beef Bake
Lynn Francisco

1 4 oz. jar sliced dry beef, separated
6 boneless, skinless chicken breast
6 strips of bacon
1 10 1/2 oz. can of cream of chicken soup

Place dried beef in 9x13 baking dish. Wrap bacon strip around each chicken breast and place over beef. In a saucepan heat chicken soup and 1/4 cup water just until it can be poured over chicken. Bake uncovered at 325 for 1 hour and 10 minutes.

Chicken and Broccoli Ring
Jill Atchley

8 count package of crescent rolls   1/2 cup mayonnaise
Small chopped onion   1 cup shredded cheese
12 ounce can of chicken (drained)
1 cup broccoli cooked, drained & chopped (fresh steamed or frozen)

Unroll the crescent rolls and layout like a clock-face layout at 12, 3, 6 & 9, then lay a second row overlapping the first. Press seams together at overlaps. Mix all other ingredients together in mixing bowl. Spoon ingredients into the area created by overlapping rolls. Roll the tips of the crescent rolls over the mixture & "tuck" under center. You should end up with a ring. Bake at the temperature & time listed on the crescent roll package. NOTE: When doubling recipe, you can still make 1 ring. Simply make your starting layer of rolls slightly farther apart. Lay the 2nd layer as usual. With the 2nd package of rolls, lay one crescent roll in between each roll from the first package.

Chicken and Cheese Enchiladas
Cleta Bailey

2 cups cooked chicken (cut up)
1 can Campbell's cheddar cheese soup
1/2 cup milk
1/2 cup chunky salsa
1 can (4 oz.) chopped green chiles
1 tsp. chili powder
8 flour tortilla

Mix milk and soup. Mix 2 Tbsp soup mixture, chicken, salsa, chiles and chili powder. Spread about 1/3 cup chicken mixture down the middle of tortilla. Roll tortilla around filling and place seam side down in greased 3 qt. casserole pan, pour remaining mixture over enchiladas. Cover and bake 375 for 35 min. or until hot.

Chicken and Spinach Pasta
Jennifer Passmore

Penne pasta, cooked
8 oz. 1 bag of fresh spinach
Rotisserie chicken from the store
1 onion
1 container chive-and-onion cream cheese
1 can diced tomatoes
Salt and pepper
1 1/2 cup shredded mozzarella cheese

Cook pasta according to package directions. Coat a frying pan with olive oil, add bag of fresh spinach on top and sauté on med. high until spinach is wilted. (You could use frozen spinach, but trust me, it is quicker and easier to cook it fresh. There is no need to drain like you would for the frozen box and the taste is awesome.) Put spinach aside and use the pan to sauté onions. Debone the Rotisserie chicken. Mix pasta, chicken, onions, spinach, cream cheese and tomatoes. Spoon mixture into a casserole dish and sprinkle top with mozzarella cheese. Bake, covered, at 375 for 30 minutes and then uncovered for 15 minutes.

Chicken and Wild Rice Casserole
Pam Herrington

1 box wild & long grain rice
2 cans of water
1 small can mushroom pieces
2 cans cream of chicken soup
1 pkg. dry onion soup mix
Desired amount of chicken pieces (boned, boneless, skin or skinless)

Mix all ingredients together. Place in loaf or small roaster pan. Lay chicken pieces on top. Bake 1 1/2 hours at 350.

Chicken Corn Casserole
Teri Henson

2 1/2 cups cooked chicken
1 small can green chiles (undrained)
1/4 cup sour cream (can use light)
1/2 cup of corn muffin mix
1/4 cup mayonnaise (can use light)
1/4 cup shredded sharp cheddar cheese
1 can (10-11 oz.) southwestern corn or any kind of Mexican-style corn, undrained
1 can (10 oz.) mild diced tomatoes (undrained)
Cooking spray

Preheat oven to 425. Spray 2 quart dish with cooking spray. Combine all ingredients except cheese in bowl. Mix well. Bake for 20 minutes. Remove from oven and sprinkle cheese over top. Bake another 5 minutes until cheese melts. Let it stand for 5 minutes before serving.

Chicken Casserole
Keith and Lee Ann Martin

3 cup chicken, cooked and cube
1/2 cup mayonnaise
1 cup cooked rice
1 sleeve Ritz crackers, crushed

1 can cr. of mushroom soup
4 tsp. lemon juice
1 small sour cream (8 oz.)
1 stick melted margarine

Mix everything except Ritz crackers and margarine. Place in 3-quart casserole. Top with mixture of margarine and cracker crumbs. Bake 45 minutes at 350. *Hint* - crush the crackers in a large zip lock bag. Easy to crush with your hands or a rolling pin!

Chicken Enchiladas
Sheila Mathis

1 10 oz. can cream of chicken soup
1 Tbsp. margarine or butter
1 t. chili powder
8 flour tortillas
1/2 cup sour cream
1/2 cup chopped onion
2 c. cooked chicken, chopped
1 cup (4 oz.) shredded jack or cheddar cheese
1 4 oz. can chopped green chiles (Rotel - diced tomatoes and peppers) drained

Mix soup and sour cream. Heat margarine in pan and add onion and the chili powder. Cook until tender. Add the chicken, chiles and 2 Tbs of the soup mixture. Add 1/2 cup cheese, stir and remove from the heat. Spread 1/2 cup of soup mixture in a 2-quart shallow baking dish. On each tortilla, spread 1/4 c. of chicken mixture, roll and arrange with seam side down in the baking dish. Spread remaining mixture over the top, especially the ends. Sprinkle remaining cheese over the top. Bake at 350 for 25 minutes.

Chicken Lasagna
Stacy Metz

3 cups cooked chicken
1 jar alfredo sauce
16 oz. ricotta cheese
1 egg
2 cups mozzarella cheese
1 pkg. lasagna - ready to cook
2 cups parmesan cheese

Mix egg, ricotta cheese, and Alfredo sauce. Add torn/shredded chicken. Spray 9x13 baking dish. Layer sauce, lasagna, mozzarella cheese, all the way to the top of the dish. Top with the parmesan cheese. Bake at 350 for 45 min.

Chicken Nuggets
Samantha Slade

3 boneless chicken breasts
1/2 cup Italian seasoned bread crumbs
1/4 cup Parmesan cheese
1/2 tsp. salt
1/2 cup butter

Preheat oven to 400. Cut each breast into nuggets. Combine bread crumbs, cheese and salt. Dip chicken nuggets in melted butter, then in crumb mixture. Place in single layer on a foil lined baking sheet. Bake at 400 for 20 minutes.

Chicken Piccata
Samantha Slade

4 boneless skinless chicken breasts
1/1/2 Tbsp. all purpose flour
2 Tbsp. olive oil
1/4 cup fresh lemon juice
1/4 can low sodium chicken broth

3 Tbsp. butter, softened
Additional all purpose flour
1/3 cup dry white wine
1/4 cup drained capers
1/4 cup fresh parsley, chopped

Place chicken breast between 2 large sheets of plastic wrap. Using a meat pounder or rolling pin, lightly pound chicken to 1/4 inch thickness. Sprinkle chicken with salt and pepper. Mix 1 Tbsp butter and 1 1/2 Tbsp flour in a small bowl until smooth. Place additional flour in a shallow baking dish. Dip chicken into flour to coat; shake off excess. Heat 1 Tbsp oil in each of 2 heavy skillets. Add 2 chicken breasts to each skillet and cook until golden and cooked through, about 3 minutes per side. Transfer chicken to platter and tent with foil to keep warm. Bring wine, lemon juice and broth to a boil in 1 skillet over medium high heat. Whisk in butter-flour mixture and boil until sauce thickens slightly, about 2 minutes. Stir in capers, parsley and remaining 2 Tbsp butter. Season sauce to taste with salt and pepper. Pour sauce over chicken and serve. Recipe can be doubled.

Chicken Pot Pie
Andreah Wellman

2 - 10 oz. cans cream of potato soup
1 15 oz. can mixed vegetables, drained
1 1/2 cups diced, cooked chicken
1/2 cup milk
A splash of sherry (optional)
1/2 tsp. each thyme, sage, and Italian seasoning
1/2 tsp. pepper
1 egg, slightly beaten, optional
2 9" pie crusts (I use Pillsbury refrigerator pie crust)

Combine first six ingredients and spoon into bottom pie crust. Cover with top pie crust, crimp edges to seal. Slit top crust, and brush with egg, if desired. Bake at 375 for 40 minutes. (This recipe can be doubled and baked in 9x13" dish)

Chicken Strips
Diana Burnside

6 oz. Tyson boneless, skinless chicken cut into 5 strips
1/2 cup Fiber One cereal (the ones that looks like sticks)
1/4 cup Egg Beaters, original
1/4 tsp. Lawry's Garlic
Salt and pepper, to taste

Preheat oven to 375. Using a blender, grind Fiber One cereal into bread crumbs. Add garlic salt and pepper. Place crumbs in one small dish and Egg Beaters in another. Next coat raw chicken with Egg Beaters and then crumbs. Place strips on a baking pan sprayed with non-stick spray. Spray a light mist of non-stick spray on the strips (top) and place in oven. Cook 10 minutes and then turn strips over. Add another light mist of spray and cook for 8-10 min. or more until done.

Chicken Tacos (family favorite and EASY!)
Betsy Hall

1 8 oz. pkg. Philadelphia cream cheese (low fat, ok) cubed.
1/3 cup milk
1 1/2 cups cooked chicken, chopped or shredded
1/2 tsp. salt
1 4 oz. can chopped green chiles, drained
10 taco shells
1/4 tsp. chili powder or ground cumin (I use chili powder)
Shredded lettuce
Chopped tomatoes

Combine cream cheese and milk in saucepan; stir over low heat until smooth. Stir in chicken, chilies and seasonings; heat thoroughly, stirring occasionally. Watch can burn and stick. Serve in taco shells with a salad or fruit. I double this so there is some for leftovers the next day or so.

Chicken Tazewell
Bill & Jannon Pierce

4 boneless skinless chicken breasts
4 slices bacon
1 can cream of mushroom soup
1 cup sour cream pepper
4 thin slices cooked Smithfield ham (Prosciutto works, also)

Sprinkle chicken with pepper (to taste). Wrap a bacon slice around each breast. Arrange ham slices in the bottom of a casserole. Place a chicken breast over each ham slice. Combine mushroom soup and sour cream, and pour over chicken. Bake, covered, at 300 for about 90 minutes. Uncover and bake for an additional thirty minutes.

Chicken Tetrazzini
Andreah Wellman

2 1/2 cups spaghetti, broken into 2" pieces
1/4 cup diced pimentos
1 large onion, chopped
1 cup chicken broth
1 tsp. salt
4 cups cut up chicken, cooked
3 1/2 cups grated sharp cheddar cheese
1/2 cup green pepper
1/2 tsp. pepper
2 cans condensed cream of mushroom soup, undiluted

Cook spaghetti and drain. Place cooked chicken, pimentos, green pepper, and onion in a 3 qt casserole, or 9x13" pan. Pour in mushroom soup and chicken broth. Add salt, pepper, 2 1/2 cups of the grated cheese, and spaghetti. Toss lightly until well mixed and spaghetti is coated with sauce. Sprinkle remaining grated cheese over the top. Bake at 350 for 1 hour, or until bubbling hot. Can be made ahead and refrigerated. Makes 8 servings.

"Dad's" Famous Steak
Terry Richards

Large top round or London broil steak, 1 1/2 to 2 in. thick.
Large bottle of Wishbone Italian Dressing

Start stabbing the steak with a fork 50 times covering both sides. Put steak in large freezer bag cover with Italian dressing and seal. Marinate in refrigerator for 2 nights. Sprinkle with Morton Nature Seasoning and a little Everglades Seasoning. Cook on the grill until medium rare. Slice thin from small end of steak.

Country Style Chicken Medley
Melanie Richards

Vegetable Mixture:

1/4 cup sweet butter
1 can of whole kernel corn, drained
1 tsp. basil leaves
4 cups peeled, sliced potatoes
1 tsp. salt
1/4 tsp. nutmeg

Chicken and crumb mixture:
Enough graham cracker crumbs to coat chicken
1 tsp. salt
1/3 cup melted butter
1 1/2 tsp. basil leaves
3 pounds frying chicken, cut into pieces

Melt 1/4 cup butter in 13x9x2 inch baking dish. Add sliced potatoes and corn. Sprinkle with 1 tsp salt 1 tsp basil and 1/4 tsp nutmeg. Set aside. Combine graham cracker crumbs, 1 tsp salt and 1 tsp basil; mix well. Dip chicken into 1/3 cup melted butter, then into crumb mixture to coat; place skin side up on top of vegetable mixture. Sprinkle with 1/2 tsp basil. Cover tightly with foil; bake in center of 375 oven for 75 minutes or until tender. Remove foil; bake for 10 minutes longer to brown. Yields 4 to 6 servings.

Dr. Martin's Mix
Brian Hall

1-1 1/2 lb. of pork sausage (Can use hamburger, but sausage is better)
2 green onions/scallions, chopped
1 green pepper, chopped
2-3 celery stalks, chopped
2 cups chicken consommé or bouillon
1 cup raw rice
1 Tbsp. Worcestershire sauce
1/2 tsp. salt

Crumble sausage in a skillet and brown. Pour off excess fat. Then add all the remaining ingredients. Put a lid on it and let it simmer on low heat. Simmer about an hour. ENJOY!

Easy Chicken Bake
Lynn Francisco

8 boneless, skinless chicken breasts
3/4 cup mayonnaise
2 cups crushed cornflake crumbs
1/4 cup grated parmesan cheese

Sprinkle chicken breasts with salt and pepper. Dip chicken in mayonnaise and spread mayonnaise over chicken with a brush. Combine cornflakes and parmesan cheese. Dip mayonnaise-covered chicken in the cornflake mixture (get plenty of the crumbs on chicken) and place on a non-stick vegetable sprayed 9x13" inch glass baking dish. Bake uncovered at 325 for 1 hour

Easy Chicken Enchiladas
Sharon Chastain

1 small, chopped Onion
1 can refried beans
12-16 oz. cooked cubed chicken
lettuce, tomato, sour cream for garnish

12 oz. pkg. cheddar cheese
1 large can enchilada sauce
8-10 flour tortillas

Mix together chicken, refried beans, onion, 1/2 cup enchilada sauce, and cheese (save some for garnish). Divide mixture equally down center of each flour tortilla and roll them up. Place seem side down in 9x11 baking dish. Top with remaining enchilada sauce and cheese. Bake 30 minutes at 350. Top with lettuce, tomato, and sour cream and serve.

Easy Lasagna
Linda Rehder

2 or 3 lbs ground beef
½ cup chopped green pepper (optional)
1 large box lasagna noodles - uncooked
1 cup parmesan cheese (fresh is best)
1 large carton cottage cheese
2 Tbsp. fresh parsley or parsley flakes
2 Tbsp. chopped fresh basil or dried basil flakes
3 cups shredded mozzarella cheese
1 small onion chopped
3 Tbsp. minced garlic
32 oz. spaghetti sauce
3/4 cup water
1 8 oz. carton Ricotta cheese

Brown ground beef, chopped onion and green pepper together. Drain all grease and add spaghetti sauce and minced garlic to meat mixture; return to stove and place on simmer. Mix following in large bowl: parmesan cheese, cottage cheese, Ricotta cheese, parsley and basil. Grease or spray a large and deep cake pan. Line bottom of pan with dry, uncooked lasagna noodles, next put a layer of ground beef mixture (about 1/3 of meat mixture); next put a layer of cottage cheese mixture and then a layer of mozzarella cheese; repeat layers ending with mozzarella cheese on top. Bake covered at 350 at least 1 hour or until noodles are tender. (take lid or foil off last 15-20 minutes). Let set out of oven at least 15 minutes before cutting.

Fried Ravioli
Jennifer Passmore

Frozen package of cheese ravioli
1 can of bread crumbs
Oil for deep frying
2 eggs
1 cup of parmesan cheese

Cook ravioli just a little under the package directions. Allow the ravioli to cool. Wisk eggs in a swallow dish. In a second shallow dish mix together bread crumbs and cheese. Dip cooled ravioli in egg mixture and then coat in bread crumbs. Deep fry breaded ravioli in 375 degree oil. Serve with marinara sauce

Easy Weeknight Rice and Chicken
Jennifer Passmore

3 cups of cooked white rice
1 can chicken soup
1 cup mayonnaise
1 cup sharp cheddar cheese
1 bag of steam microwave broccoli
Rotisserie Chicken
2 sleeves of buttery crackers
4 Tbsp. of butter

Cook rice according to package directions. Cook broccoli. Debone chicken. Mix soup, mayo, broccoli, cheese and chicken. Spoon into a casserole dish. Crush crackers and sprinkle on top. Melt butter and pour on top of casserole. Bake at 350 for 30 minutes.

Easy Yellow Rice and Chicken
Jennifer Passmore

Rotisserie chicken
1 pkg. yellow rice mix
2 1/2 cups of chicken stock
2 Tbsp. olive oil

Follow the cooking instructions for the rice according to package directions except substitute chicken stock for water. Pull the chicken off the bones and tear up into pieces that are a little bigger than bite size. Ten minutes before the rice is cooked add the chicken. If you want the ids to be lower in fat, do not put any of the skin in the rice. When the rice is done you are ready to serve. I always serve it with green peas. It is the only way I can get my husband to ever eat peas, he mixes them up with rice. Buttered Cuban bread is always perfect with this dish

Fried Chicken
Terry Richards

5 boneless chicken breast
All purpose, pre-sifted flour
3 eggs

Gravy:
1 1/2 cups water
3 chicken bullion cubes
2 Tbs. flour

Gravy for chicken: skim grease off drippings in pan after making fried chicken. Add 1 1/2 cups water, 3 chicken bullion cubes, put 2 Tbsp flour in 1/2 cup water. Stir until blended add to drippings. Stir while heating to bubbling, turn down to simmer, stir until thick. Add pepper to taste.
In electric frying pan or frying pan with lid on stove...add canola oil to cover bottom of pan, heat to medium high heat. Beat eggs in bowl, put flour in another bowl. Dip chicken in egg and then coat both sides with flour. Put chicken in hot oil season with Morton Nature's Seasoning. Let cook 5 minutes on one side. Turn over and brown both sides until chicken is done (about 25 mins.) Chicken is done when fork goes in and comes out easily. Or cut in half and check, like I do.

Hamburger & Rice Tonight!
Teresa Harvey

1-2 lbs. ground beef
1 can cream of mushroom Soup
1-2 cups Minute Rice (uncooked)
1 small onion diced
1 can water
Salt and pepper, to taste

Mix all together in a lightly sprayed 9x13 baking dish. Bake for 30 to 40 minutes until rice appears to be done.

Grandmas Easy Chicken Casserole
Lara Lynn

3 Chicken Breasts
3 cans Rotel tomatoes
corn chips

2 cans cream of chicken soup
1 1/2 cups shredded cheddar

Preheat oven to 375. Boil chicken, when cooked set aside to cool. Then, cut into bite size. Add chicken, soup, and Rotel to a 13x9 in baking dish. Cook for 45 minutes. Top with cheese for last 5 minutes. Serve with corn chips.

Grilled Marinated Salmon
Samantha Slade

1/4 cup pineapple juice
2 Tbsp. brown sugar
1/8 tsp. garlic powder
1 lb. salmon fillet

2 Tbsp. soy sauce
1/2 tsp. fresh cracked pepper
1/2 cup vegetable oil

Combine all ingredients except salmon. Remove all skin from salmon. Place salmon in a Ziploc bag and pour marinade over it. Refrigerate hours or for more flavor refrigerate overnight. Heat grill to medium high. Drain salmon and cook approx. 5 minutes each side. I find it's less messy to cook the fish on aluminum foil that has been sprayed with non-stick cooking spray.

Grilled Bruschetta Chicken
Cleta Bailey

1/4 cup Kraft sun-dried tomato vinaigrette dressing divided
4 small boneless chicken breast (about 1 lb.)
1 tomato, finely chopped
1/2 cup mozzarella cheese
1/4 cup chopped fresh basil or 1 tsp. dry basil leaves

Place large sheet heavy duty foil over half of grill. Preheat grill to medium heat. Pour 2 tsp dressing over chicken in resealable plastic bag; seal bag. Turn bag to coat. Chicken with dressing. Refrigerate 10 min. to marinate. Remove chicken. Discard bag and marinade. Grill chicken on uncovered side of grill 6 min. Meanwhile combine tomatoes, cheese, basil and remaining 2 Tbsp dressing. Turn chicken over; place cooked side up, on foil on grill. Top evenly with tomato mixture. Close lid. Grill an additional 8 min. or until chicken is cooked through. Enjoy with cooked spaghetti and grilled or steamed veggies.

Italian Chicken and Rice
Beth Cowart

1-1/2 cups water
1 cup uncooked rice
1 can (14 1/2 oz.) tomatoes cut up, undrained
1/2 lb. VELVEETA cheese spread, diced
1/4 cup finely chopped onion
1-1/2 tsp. Italian seasonings divided
1(2 to 3lb.) broiler fryer cut up, skinned
2/3 cup grated parmesan cheese

Preheat oven to 375. Stir together water, rice, cheese spread, onions and tsp Italian seasonings into greased 13x9 inch baking dish. Top with chicken: sprinkle with parmesan cheese and remaining Italian seasonings. Bake 455 to 50 minutes or until chicken is tender. Let stand 5 minutes 4 to 6 servings.

Italian Crescent Bake
Dot Ann Erickson

1 ½ lb. ground beef
½ cup chopped onion
8 oz. can tomato sauce
1/2 cup sour cream
1/4 tsp. oregano
1 cup sliced mushrooms
1/2 tsp. salt and pepper
1 c. (4 oz.) shredded cheddar cheese
8 oz. can refrigerator crescent rolls
1/4 tsp. rosemary

In frying pan brown ground beef, mushrooms and onion; drain. Add salt, pepper and tomato sauce. Place in ungreased 8x12 baking pan and sprinkle with cheese. (You can make this part ahead and refrigerate.) Separate dough into 8 triangles. Combine sour cream and spices. Spread 1 tsp mixture on each triangle. Roll up starting at wide end. Arrange on top of casserole. Bake at 350 for 25-30 minutes or until golden brown.
You can make this a lower calorie dish by using very lean ground beef, fat free sour cream, lower fat cheese and light crescent rolls. It is still very delicious!

Juiciest Hamburgers Ever
Rae Sprow

2 pounds ground beef
1 egg, beaten
3/4 cup dry Italian-style bread crumbs
5 tablespoons Hickory Brown Sugar Barbecue Sauce
1 pat of butter for each hamburger

Preheat grill for high heat. In a large bowl, mix the ground beef, egg, bread crumbs, and barbecue sauce. Form the mixture into 8 hamburger patties. Make a dent in center of each patty and place a small pat of butter. Close by spreading meat over butter. Lightly oil the grill grate. Grill patties 5 minutes per side, or until well done.

Jake's Boss Barbecue Rub
Kelly Beale

1 1/4 cups packed dark brown sugar
1/4 cup kosher or sea salt
1/2 cup paprika
3 Tbsp. dried parsley
2 Tbsp. dried basil
2 Tbsp. dried oregano
2 Tbsp. dried thyme
2 Tbsp. dried onion flakes
1 1/2 Tbsp. lemon pepper
1 Tbsp. garlic powder
1 tsp. ground allspice
1 tsp. ground cinnamon

Combine all the ingredients in a bowl and stir or whisk to mix. Transfer to a large jar, cover, and store away from heat and light. The Rub will keep for several months. Great on salmon, chicken, steaks, or chops.

Just-A-Moment Mexican Skillet
Kelly Willard

1 lb. mild pork sausage, browned
2 Tbsp. sugar
Chili powder to taste
1 cup small pasta shells
28 oz. can petite diced tomatoes
Miracle Whip to taste

Brown sausage, rinse & drain. Add sugar, chili powder, tomatoes, pasta, and a little water as necessary for pasta to absorb. Boil, then simmer until pasta is cooled. Add Miracle Whip to taste. Serve with grated parmesan.

Lasagna
Cam Webb

2 cans stewed tomatoes (Italian recipe)
1 can tomato sauce
1 can tomato paste
1 clove garlic
1 box lasagna noodles
1 sm. carton Ricotta cheese
1 pkg. Swiss cheese
1 pkg. mozzarella cheese
1 lb. lean ground beef

Brown lean ground beef, add stewed tomatoes, tomato sauce & tomato paste, clove garlic (3-4 pieces) Simmer for an hour. Cook lasagna noodles. In casserole dish layer noodles, ricotta cheese, sauce, mozzarella cheese & Swiss cheese. Continue layers until ingredients are used. Bake at 350 for 1/2 hr or until bubbles. Can be made a day in advance & refrigerated. Or freeze for future baking & serving.

Lisa's Perfect Sausage & Pasta Bake
Lisa Bua

1 lb. Italian sausage links, cut into 1/4 in. slices
1 jar spaghetti sauce
8 oz. mostaccioli, cooked & drained
1/3 cup grated parmesan
1 pkg. (4oz.) shredded mozzarella

In a large skillet, brown sausage until no longer pink. Drain. In a greased 2 qt baking dish combine the sausage, sauce, mostacciloi, and parmesan cheese. Top with mozzarella cheese. Bake a 350, for 15 minutes or until heated through.

Marinated Grilled Chicken
Rae Sprow

This is my favorite way to grill chicken. The chicken turns out so tender and moist!

4 skinless, boneless chicken breast halves
1 (16 oz.) bottle Zesty Italian-style salad dressing
1/4 tsp. lemon pepper
 Salt to taste

Rinse chicken and pat dry. Pound chicken, then place in a shallow glass bowl and pour 1/2 bottle of salad dressing over it. Cover and refrigerate for at least 3 hours or overnight. Lightly oil grill and preheat to medium high. Remove chicken breasts from marinade. Season with lemon pepper and salt to taste. Grill over medium high heat for 10 to 15 minutes on each side, or until chicken is cooked through and juices run clear.

Ms. Pam's Easiest Entrée
Pam Patterson

6 red skin potatoes, cut in chunks
2 Tbsp. olive oil
Hillshire smoke sausage, sliced
1/2 cup onion, diced
Complete Seasoning (found in the Latino section at the grocery store)

Heat olive oil over medium to medium-high heat in skillet. Add all ingredients. Flavor to taste with Complete Seasoning. Cook 15-20 minutes or until done.

Meat Loaf
Janice Sprowles

1 1/2 lb. ground beef
1 cup seasoned breadcrumbs
1 onion diced
1 egg, lightly beaten
1 tsp. salt
1/2 tsp. pepper
3/4 cup pizza sauce or spaghetti sauce
2 Tbsp. vinegar
3 Tbsp. brown sugar
2 Tbsp. Dijon mustard
2 tablespoon Worcestershire sauce
1/2 cup pizza sauce or spaghetti sauce

Preheat oven to 350. Mix together the beef, breadcrumbs, onion, egg, salt, pepper and 3/4 cup of pizza sauce. Shape into a loaf and place in shallow pan. Stir together the 1/2 cup pizza sauce, vinegar, sugar, mustard and Worcestershire. Pour sauce over meatloaf. Bake for 1 hour.

Meat Loaf Meal
Peggy Butz

Combine in a large bowl:
1 1/2 pounds lean ground beef
2/3 cup milk
2 teaspoons Worcestershire sauce
1/4 tsp. pepper

1/3 cup soft bread crumbs
1/4 cup catsup
1 tsp. salt

Mix well. Shape into a loaf in center of a 13x9x2 inch baking dish.

Peel and slice 1/4 inch thick:
3 medium potatoes
Peel and quarter lengthwise:
Combine 2 tsp. dry parsley flakes
Set aside.

3 medium onions
3 carrots
1 tsp. salt dash pepper

Arrange onions AROUND meat loaf and sprinkle with 1/3 of the parsley mixture. Arrange potatoes over onion and sprinkle with another 1/3 of the parsley mixture. Top with carrots. Sprinkle remainder of parsley mixture over all. Cover tightly with aluminum foil. Bake at 375 for 1 hour, or until vegetables are tender. Uncover and bake 10 minutes longer to brown meat.

Nachos
Tom, Debi, and Kathy Jo Cole

1 lb. ground beef
1 can 16-oz. refried beans
1 can Rotel diced tomatoes and green chilies
16 oz. Pace picante sauce
8 to 12 oz. Mexican shredded cheese
1 large bag nacho chips
 Jalapenos peppers (optional) black olives (optional) mushrooms (optional)

Preheat oven to 350 degree. Crush nacho chips on a pizza pan and set aside. Cook ground beef and drain oil. Add the Rotel tomatoes and green chilies and refried beans. Cook until the beans, beef and Rotel are like a sauce. Pour the ground beef, refried beans, and Rotel over the nacho chips and spread it out covering the nachos. Pour the Pace picante and spread over the ground beef, refried beans and Rotel. Spread the shredded cheese over the top and place optional items over the cheese. Back in the oven for 15 min.

Orange Chicken
Stacy Metz

1 cup lite soy sauce
1 tsp. powdered ginger
3 - 4 garlic cloves, peeled and crushed
2 liter bottle orange flavored soda
10 - 15 chicken thighs, skinned

Brown chicken in Dutch-oven with garlic. Drain excess oil from pan and add remaining ingredients. Simmer on med-low heat about 25 minutes until liquid runs clear from thigh when pierced near the bone. Enjoy!

Mexican Pizza
Mike Wilder

Crust:
2 boxes corn muffin mix
2 eggs
4 Tbsp. melted butter
1 1/2 cups milk
1 cup frozen corn kernels
Extra-virgin olive oil or, vegetable oil, for drizzling

Topping
2 Tbsp. extra-virgin or vegetable oil, 2 turns of the pan
1 lb. ground beef
1 small onion, finely chopped
1 Tbsp. chili powder
2 tsp. ground cumin
2 tsp. cayenne sauce
Salt, to taste
2 1/2 cups shredded cheddar or jack cheese
1/2 red bell pepper, chopped
1 small can, 2 1/4 ounces sliced chiles or jalapenos, drained
2 scallions, chopped
2 small vine ripe tomatoes, seeded and diced
2 Tbsp. drained sliced green olives (salad   olives)
1 to 2 Tbsp. chopped cilantro leaves, optional garnish
Mild to medium taco sauce to pass at table, 1 cup

Preheat oven to 400 degrees . Mix together 2 packages muffin mix with 2 eggs, 4 tablespoons melted butter (melt in microwave 30 seconds), 1 1/2 cups milk and frozen corn kernels. Wipe a nonstick skillet with a little extra or vegetable oil and pour in the muffin mix. Use a large skillet, 10 to 12 inch. Choose a pan with oven safe handle or, double-wrap handle with foil to protect it in the oven. Place pan in oven and bake 12 to 15 minutes in center of the oven until light golden in color. Brown the meat over medium high heat in a second skillet in extra or vegetable oil, 2 turns of the pan. Add onions and spices and cook meat 5 minutes more. Remove cornbread from oven and top with meat, cheese, and veggies. Add pan back to oven and cook 5 minutes more to melt cheese. Garnish with cilantro, optional. Cut into 8 wedges and serve the deep dish pan pizza from the skillet. Pass taco sauce at the table to sprinkle on top.

No Ordinary Crab Cake
Kelly Beale

1 lb. Jumbo Lump crabmeat, drained (16 oz. each)
1 lb. special crabmeat drained
1/2 green pepper diced
2 Tbsp. Old Bay Seasoning
2 Tbsp. Dijon mustard
1 Tbsp. lemon juice
1 Tbsp. Worcestershire sauce
1 1/2 -2 cups bread crumbs

1/2 red pepper, diced
1/4 onion diced
1/2 cup mayonnaise
2 egg whites
1 Tbsp. soy sauce
2 dashes Tabasco sauce

Sweat vegetables. Cook until just softened. Once vegetables are cooked, add Old Bay Seasoning. Mix wet ingredients (mayo, mustard, egg whites, lemon juice, soy sauce, Worcestershire, and Tabasco) together. Add vegetables and Old Bay mixture to wet ingredients. Combine wet ingredients and vegetables with crabmeat. Add 2 cups bread crumbs. Mix. Allow mixture to rest for 10 - 15 mins for the bread crumbs to soak up liquid. Add more bread crumbs if needed. Scoop as needed. Sauté on each side for 5 mins until golden brown.

Old Fashion Roast Beef
Lynn Francisco

1 3-5 lb. chuck roast flour canola oil
1 onion
2 potatoes chopped
1 bag of baby carrots
Salt, pepper, garlic salt, garlic powder
Everglades Seasoning

In Dutch-oven heat oil. Season roast and then flour roast. Brown roast in hot oil on both sides. Take out and pour oil out of Dutch-oven. I use a meat rack and set roast with sliced onion on top on rack. Pour 1 cup of water in pan and cook at 275 for 6-8 hours. Put potatoes and carrots in after about 3 hours. Yummy!

Panko Crusted Chicken
Jennifer Passmore

1 can cream of chicken soup
1/2 cup mayonnaise
1 1/2 cups Panko bread crumbs
1 cup cheddar cheese
5 boneless, skinless, chicken breast
1 cup flour
1/2 cup butter softened

Mix soup and mayo. Dust chicken with flour and place chicken in a casserole dish. Coat each chicken with mixture. Mix Panko crumbs, soft butter and cheese. Top chicken with Panko mixture. Cover with foil and bake for 10 minutes at 425. Uncover and bake for 15 more minutes until chicken is done.

Penne with Sun-Dried Tomato Pesto
Jennifer Passmore

1 jar sundried tomato
1 cup fresh basil
2 cloves of garlic
1/2 cup parmesan
Salt
Pasta

Add jar of sundried tomato and oil the tomatoes were packaged in, garlic, salt, and basil to a food processor and blend. Stir in the parmesan cheese. Cook pasta according to package directions. Add pasta to pesto and toss. Add a 1/4 to 1/2 of cup of the pasta water to pasta to thin out and allow pesto to coat the pasta.

Perfectly Easy Parmesan Chicken
Kim Earley

4-6 chicken breasts	2 eggs
1 sleeve of Ritz crackers	1-2 Tbsp. garlic cloves, crushed
1 cup grated parmesan cheese	1-2 tsp. lemon juice
1 stick of butter	

Crush crackers into crumbs in a Ziploc bag with rolling pin. Add the parmesan cheese. Mix the two together. Pour on to a large plate. Whip eggs and put on a separate large plate. Coat chicken with egg and then roll in cracker/cheese mix. Put into 9x13 pan . Melt butter in microwave, add garlic and then lemon juice. Pour over chicken. Bake for 35-40 minutes at 350 degrees.

Porcupine Meatballs
Chris Wellman

1-1/2 lbs ground beef   1/2 cup regular rice
2/3 cup milk   1 1/2 tsp. salt
1 Tbsp. instant minced, or 1 medium onion, finely chopped
1/4 tsp. pepper   1/4 tsp. garlic powder
1 can condensed tomato soup   3/4 cup water

Combine ground beef, rice, milk, minced onion, salt, pepper, and garlic powder in bowl. Mix well with hands or spoon. Drop rounded Tablespoonfuls of mixture into 13x9x2 inch baking pan. Combine tomato soup and water in bowl. Mix well. Pour over meatball. Cover baking pan tightly with aluminum foil. Bake in 350 degree oven 1 hour or until hot and bubbly, and rice is poking out of meatballs. Makes 6 - 8 servings. Spoon tomato gravy over each meatball.

Pork Chops & Rice
Reba Pearson

Pork Chops Large   Can of Chicken & Rice Soup

Crock Pot Recipe Brown Pork Chops (Cook just to brown) Add chicken & Rice Soup Cook in Crock Pot 6-8 hours

Pork Chop Casserole
Jannon Pierce

3-4 medium thick pork chops   Salt & Pepper
2-3 lbs of potatoes   1/2 onion
2 Campbell's mushroom soup (Do not use thin soup brands)

Cube potatoes. Dice onions. Mix all ingredients except pork and place in a Pyrex dish. Lay pork chops on top. Bake for 1-1.5 hours until potatoes are done (knife tender).

Roast Marinade
Wilhelmina Ellermets

1 tsp. Accent
2 Tbsp. cooking oil
1/4 cup ketchup
1 Tbsp. mustard
1 tsp. salt

1/3 cup wine vinegar
1 Tbsp. Worcestershire sauce
2 Tbsp. soy sauce
1/2 Tbsp. garlic powder
1/4 tsp. pepper

Sprinkle roast or steak with Accent. Place in shallow dish. Combine all ingredients and pour over the meat. Marinade 2-3 hours. It flavors and tenderizes the meat. Turn it over once or twice. Place roast or steaks on grill - 6 inches from heat. Turn and baste again. Grill roast to medium or medium rare, slice roast super thin. Steaks need about 5 minutes on each side. This marinade always gets raves from our guest! God Bless!

Robert's 20-20-20 Roast
Andreah Wellman

1 eye of round roast, any size   Olive oil
1 package McCormick Montreal Steak Seasoning

Place aluminum foil in the bottom of a 9x13" pan. Rub olive oil on all sides. Sprinkle the steak seasoning over roast and rub on all sides. Place seasoned roast on aluminum lined pan. Bake at 500 degrees for 20 min. Don't open oven door. Turn oven off, and leave in for 20 minutes. Again, don't open oven door. When time is up, remove roast from oven and let it sit for 20 min. on top of stove or counter. This roast will be more on the med-rare side. If you like your meat more done, increase time to 23-23-23, or 25-25-25, but no longer.

Roquefort Chicken
Bill & Jannon Pierce

Chicken:
Three to four boneless/skinless breasts
2 Tbsp. butter
Sourdough bread crumbs
Olive oil
Parmesan cheese
1 cup milk
Worcestershire sauce
salt and pepper
thyme

Sauce:
3 stalks celery
1-2 shallots
1 can chicken broth
White wine
16 oz. cream (light or heavy as desired)
8 oz. Roquefort (or other favorite blue cheese)
Chives to taste

Sauce:
Sauté three stalks celery and 1-2 shallots in butter 2 minutes. Add one can chicken broth and equal amount white wine. Reduce slowly to one tablespoon of liquid. Discard shallots and celery. Add 16 oz. of cream and 8 oz. of Roquefort or other blue cheese. Cook on very low heat until blue cheese melts.(Add more cheese if sauce is not thick enough). Add chives 30 seconds before sauce is to be poured over chicken.

Chicken:
Make sourdough bread crumbs by toasting six sourdough bread slices and then running the slices through a food processor. Lightly coat a baking dish with olive oil, then put 1/2 of the bread crumbs in the bottom of the dish. Sprinkle with thyme and parmesan cheese; season to taste with salt and pepper (I use white pepper, but black will do.) Dip each chicken breast in a mixture of milk, 2 tbsp. melted butter, and Worcestershire sauce for chicken; then lay breasts on bread crumb mixture. Place the remainder of the bread crumbs on the chicken (cover completely), and season the top with thyme, parmesan cheese, salt, and pepper. Bake covered approximately 40 minutes on 375 degrees. Spoon sauce over chicken. Caution: Because this is a cream sauce, it does not make great leftovers.

Ruth's Brisket & Susie's Barbecue Sauce
Sandy Taylor

Brisket
1 5 lb. beef brisket, trimmed of excess fat
2 tsp. garlic salt
2 tsp. celery salt
5 Tbsp. Liquid Smoke
1 bottle (2.5oz.) Worcestershire sauce
2 tsp. onion salt
1 med. onion, minced
1/4 tsp. pepper

Sauce
1 bottle (32oz.) ketchup
1/2 c. firmly packed brown sugar
1 tsp. garlic salt
2 dashes bottled red pepper sauce
1 tsp. chili powder
1/4 tsp. ground red pepper
2 c. water
1/4 c. Worcestershire sauce
2 Tbsp. vinegar
1 dry mustard
1 Tbsp. + 2 tsp. liquid smoke
1 1/4 tsp. coarse black pepper

Place brisket in a 9x13 inch baking dish or cast-iron pot, fat side down. Sprinkle on remaining ingredients except Worcestershire sauce and pepper. Cover with foil and refrigerate overnight. Next day, sprinkle Worcestershire sauce and pepper over brisket. Preheat oven to 275F. Bake covered 6 hours. Remove from sauce and shred or slice meat. Pour on 2 cups Susie's Barbecue Sauce and serve warm. Makes 10 servings, about 535 calories each. Sauce in large saucepan combine all ingredients. Cook over medium heat; let simmer 40-45 minutes, stirring occasionally. Pour into quart jars and store in refrigerator. Makes about 6 cups, about 8 calories per tablespoon.

Santa Fe Chicken
Licia White

4 boneless, skinless chicken breast
1 jar (14 oz.)salsa
1 handful of shredded cheddar cheese
1 15 oz. can black beans
1 small can of corn

Place chicken in a 9x11 casserole pan. Put on top of chicken the beans, salsa, and corn. (mix together lightly) Bake at 350 for about 45 min. (until chicken is done). 5 min. before ready sprinkle with cheese. Suggested: Serve with corn bread and rice.

Seafood Lasagna
Pam Herrington

1 lb. reduced fat cream cheese
1/4 cup milk
3 scallions - trimmed and chopped
2 tsp. Old Bay or Creole seasoning
2 sweet red peppers - cored, seeded & finely diced
2 boxes (10 oz.) frozen, chopped broccoli - thawed, squeezed, dried
3/4 cup imitation crab meat, shredded
2 eggs   1/2 tsp. salt
1/4 tsp. black pepper
1 jar (1 lb.) alfredo pasta sauce
12 no-boil lasagna noodles 1/4 cup grated parmesan cheese

Heat oven to 350. Coat 9 x 13 baking dish with non stick spray. Stir cream cheese, scallions, milk and seasoning in bowl until smooth. Stir in peppers, (reserving 1/2 cup) and broccoli (reserving 1 cup). Add crabmeat, 1 egg, salt and pepper. Whisk remaining eggs into alfredo sauce. Spread 1/3 cup alfredo sauce into baking dish. Top with noodles, 1/3 of the crab meat mixture and 1/4 of alfredo sauce. Repeat layering twice. Top with 3 noodles - Sprinkle with reserved red peppers and broccoli. Pour on remaining alfredo sauce. Sprinkle with parmesan Bake, covered, at 350 for 30 min Uncover and bake and additional 20-25 min until brown and bubbly Let stand for 10 min.

Shrimp and Tortellini in Cheese Sauce
Don Bailey

1 lb. large shrimp
1 16 oz. jar of parmesan cheese sauce
2 green onions, chopped
1/2 cup white wine
1 tsp. Heart Healthy seasoning (Italian)
1 lb. three cheese tortellini
1 Roma tomato, diced
1 Tbsp. garlic
2 Tbsp. olive oil
Italian bread

Cook tortellini in salted water for 6-8 mins. Drain and set aside. In large skillet, add olive oil and shrimp and cook until shrimp is pink (do not overcook). Add garlic, onions, tomatoes and seasoning. Simmer 2 minutes until onions are cooked. Add cheese sauce and white wine and simmer until hot. Serve with tossed salad with sun-dried tomato dressing and a green vegetable or corn-on-the-cob. Use Italian bread to dip up the excess sauce. YUMMY!!!!

Shrimp with Artichokes
Pam Herrington

1 lb. large shrimp, peeled and de-veined
1 1/2 Tbsp. dried red pepper flakes
2 cups diced tomatoes
2 Tbsp. chopped fresh flatleaf parsley
1 (14 oz.) can of quartered artichoke hearts, drained
1 Tbsp. olive oil
2 garlic cloves, minced
1 tsp. paprika
1/4 tsp. salt

Heat oil in a large non-stick skillet over medium-high heat. Add shrimp, pepper flakes and garlic; sauté three minutes. Add remaining ingredients; cook three minutes, stirring frequently or until shrimp are done and mixture is thoroughly heated. Makes four servings. Best served with a big hunk of crusty bread.

Seven Layer Gratin
Pam Herrington

3 med zucchini - cut diagonally into 1/4 inch slices
1 yellow squash - cut as above
1/4 cup plus 2 Tbsp. dried bread crumbs
1 1/4 tsp. salt
1 can (8.5 oz.) artichoke hearts, drained
1 scallion, trimmed and minced
1 1/2 cups shredded Swiss cheese
1/2 tsp. dried sage
1 Tbsp. flour
1/2 tsp. black pepper
3/4 cup light cream
1/2 lb. ground turkey
2 Tbsp. grated parmesan cheese

Heat oven to 350. In lg bowl mix zucchini, yellow squash, 1/4 cup of the bread crumbs, sage, flour, 1 tsp of the salt and pepper. In blender puree artichoke hearts, scallion, 1/2 cup of Swiss cheese, 1/4 cup of the cream then remaining salt and a pinch of pepper. Spread 1/3 of squash mixture over bottom of shallow 2 quart baking dish. Spread half of the artichoke puree over squash. Top with half of the turkey. Repeat layering - top with the remaining squash mixture. Toss together remaining 1 cup Swiss cheese, remaining bread crumbs and parmesan Sprinkle evenly over gratin. Drizzle with remaining 1/2 cup light cream Bake at 350 for 50 minutes or until squash is tender and top is golden. Let stand 10 min before serving

Stuffed Chicken
Julia Baron

4 chicken breast (boneless, skinless)
1 1/2 cups fresh spinach leaves
4 slices of Havarti or smoked Gouda cheese
1 10 oz. sun dried tomato pesto sauce & spread (Classico brand)

Between plastic wrap pound cut chicken breast one at a time until about 1/2" thick. Place on slice of cheese and few leaves of spinach at one end of the chicken, then roll up. Place seam side down on a greased casserole dish. Spoon/spread pesto sauce all over top and sides of chicken. Bake at 400 uncovered for 20 min. ENJOY!

Simple Shepherd's Chicken Pie
Tara Coddington

2 pkgs. pre-cooked roasted chicken
1 pkg. prepared mashed potatoes (or 3 cups instant mashed potatoes)
1 can cream of chicken soup
1-2 cups shredded cheddar cheese
1/2 cup chopped onions
1 Tbsp. olive oil
1 tsp. Worcestershire sauce
1 tsp. minced garlic

Sauté chicken, onions, and garlic in olive oil for 3-5 minutes. Stir in Worcestershire sauce. Pour into 8x8 pan. Add the can of soup and stir well. Spread evenly in pan. Spoon mashed potatoes on top spreading evenly. Top with shredded cheese. Bake at 350 degrees for 15-20 minutes or until cheese melts. Can broil last 3-5 minutes to brown cheese.

Simply Chicken Stuffing Bake
Jane Goodbrad

1 can (10 3/4oz.) condensed cream of mushroom soup
1 cup milk
1 pkg. (6 oz.) stuffing mix
2 cups cubed cooked chicken
2 cups cooked broccoli florets
2 celery ribs, finely chopped
1 1/2 cups (6 oz.) shredded Swiss cheese

In a large bowl, combine soup and milk until blended. Add the stuffing mix with the contents of seasoning packet, chicken, broccoli, celery and 1 cup of cheese. Transfer to a greased 13x9 baking dish. Bake uncovered at 375 degrees for 20 minutes or until heated through. Sprinkle with remaining cheese; bake 5 minutes longer or until cheese is melted.

Southern Poppy-Seed Chicken
Marge Wise

3 lb. chicken, cooked and boned to make 3 to 4 cups of bite-size chicken pieces (I often cook 2 chickens so I will have leftovers for this recipe)
1 can cream of chicken soup
8 oz. lite sour cream
1 stick melted butter
1 1/2 cups crushed Ritz crackers
1 tsp. poppy seeds

Combine chicken, soup and sour cream. In a 1 1/2 qt. greased shallow casserole, arrange the chicken mixture. Combine the butter, crackers and poppy seeds. Sprinkle over chicken mixture. Bake at 350 degrees for 30 to 45 minutes or until hot. Enjoy!

Stuffed Peppers
Heather Boswell

1 lb. ground beef or turkey
1/2 cup uncooked long grain rice
6 peppers (red, green or yellow)
1 tsp. Italian seasoning
Mozzarella cheese to top (as desired)
1 cup water
1 Tbsp. Worcestershire sauce
1/4 tsp. garlic powder
Salt & pepper, to taste
2 oz. tomato sauce

Bring water to a boil then pour rice in. Reduce heat cover and cook for about 20 min. Brown ground meat and rinse when finished. Clean out the inside of peppers, place in baking dish. (Slice bottom of peppers to make them stand better, if necessary.) Mix meat, rice, 1 can tomato sauce, Worcestershire sauce, garlic powder, salt and pepper. Spoon equal amounts in the peppers. Mix remaining tomato sauce and Italian seasoning and pour over peppers. Cover with foil and bake at 350 for 55 min. Remove foil and sprinkle with desired amount of Mozzarella cheese and bake for additional 5 min.

Stuffed Green Peppers
Linda Rehder

4-6 Very large green pepper (core them from the top & dig out the seeds and white core and set aside)
Cook 2 cups of cooked rice set aside

Brown together:
2 lbs of ground beef   1 small onion chopped finely
1 cup finely chopped celery   2 Tbsp. Italian seasoning
4 Tbsp. minced garlic   Salt and pepper
Add:
2 or more cups of chunky salsa
1 can drained Italian diced tomatoes
1 lb. of Velveeta Cheese

Cook until cheese is fully melted. Fold in the cooked rice with meat mixture. Set peppers in a baking dish so they fit tightly together to prevent them from falling over. Stuff the peppers with the meat mixture. Bake at 350 - until peppers are thoroughly cooked, approximately 45-60 min.

Sweet & Sour Chicken or Ribs
Durst Family

1 8 oz. bottle apricot jam
1 bottle Red Russian salad dressing
1 envelope Lipton dry Onion Soup Mix

Combine in small saucepan - simmer 5 minutes. Arrange chicken or ribs on lightly greased 9x13 pan. Pour sauce over meat. Cover & marinate 6-8 hours in refrigerator. Do not drain. Bake at 350 for 1 1/2 hours. (or 25 minutes in microwave)

Sweet and Sour Meatballs
Laura Torrisi

1 ½ pounds ground beef	1 tablespoon shortening
2/3 cup cracker crumbs	2 tablespoons cornstarch
1/3 cup minced onion	1/2 cup brown sugar (packed)
1 egg	1/3 cup chopped green pepper
1 can (14 ounces) pineapple tidbits , drained (reserve syrup)	
1 ½ tsp. salt	1/3 cup vinegar
1/4 cup milk; for meatballs	1 Tbsp. soy sauce

Mix thoroughly beef, crumbs, onion, egg, salt, ginger and milk. Shape mixture by rounded tablespoonfuls into balls. Melt shortening in large skillet; brown and cook meatballs. Remove meatballs: keep warm Pour fat from skillet

Mix cornstarch and sugar. Stir in reserved pineapple syrup, vinegar, and soy sauce until smooth. Pour into skillet: cook over medium heat, stirring constantly, until mixture thickens and boils. Boil and stir 1 minute. Add meatballs, pineapple tidbits and green pepper heat through

Tilapia with Horseradish and Herb-Spiked Mayo
Pam Herrington

1 lemon 4 (6 oz.) tilapia fillets	1/2 tsp. garlic powder
Salt and freshly ground pepper	1/3 cup light mayonnaise
2 tsp. prepared horseradish, to taste	2 Tbsp. chopped fresh chives
2 Tbsp. chopped fresh parsley leaves	

Preheat broiler. Coat a large baking sheet with cooking spray. Finely grate 1 tsp of zest from the lemon and set aside. Squeeze the juice from the lemon over both sides of the fish. Season both sides of the fish with salt, pepper and garlic powder to taste. Place the fish on the prepared baking sheet and broil until fork-tender, about 3 minutes per side. Meanwhile, in a medium bowl, combine the mayonnaise, lemon zest, horseradish, chives, and parsley. Serve the fish with the mayonnaise mixture spooned over the top.

Taco Ring
Jill Atchley

2 packages of crescent rolls
1 lb. ground beef
Small chopped onion
1 cup prepared salsa
1 cup shredded cheese
Garnish- lettuce, tomato, sour cream, etc.

Pizza pan or cookie sheet is ideal. Unroll the crescent rolls and layout like a clock-face layout at 12, 3, 6 & 9, then lay a second row overlapping the first. With the 2nd package of rolls, lay one crescent roll in between each roll from the first package. Press seams together at overlaps. Cook ground beef & onion, drain. Add salsa and cheese. Spoon ingredients into the area created by overlapping rolls. Roll the tips of the crescent rolls over the mixture & "tuck" under center. You should end up with a ring. Bake at the temperature & time listed on the crescent roll package.

Totally Easy Tortellini Margarita
Lois Corl

1 bag frozen cheese tortellini
1/4 cup olive oil
1 large clove garlic (to taste)
1 cup diced tomatoes
1/4-1/2 cup coarsely graded parmesan
1/2 cup fresh basil leaves, neatly cut

Mince garlic and mix with olive oil. Heat in microwave for 30 seconds. Cook tortellini in boiling water for 3 minutes. Gently drain. Immediately add garlic and olive oil mix. Toss thoroughly. Add tomato & parmesan. Toss gently. Add basil right before serving. Serve with Caesar salad and crusty baguettes.

Turkey Meatloaf
Stacy Metz

1-1 1/2 lbs of ground turkey
1/4 cup low fat milk
2 slices bread torn up
1 egg, lightly beaten
Onion and garlic powder, to taste
Salt and pepper, to taste
1/4 cup ketchup for top of meatloaf

Combine all ingredients in large bowl, except for ketchup. Place in bread pan that has been sprayed with a non-stick spray. Bake at 375, for 45-60 min. or until meat is cooked throughout..

Upside Down Pizza Casserole
Linda Rehder

3 lbs ground beef
1/2 cup chopped onion
1/2 cup chopped green pepper
1 26 oz. jar of Ragu spaghetti sauce (may add tomato sauce if too dry)
2 small cans of sliced mushrooms or 1-2 cup fresh mushrooms
Black olives sliced (optional)
3 cups mozzarella cheese, shredded
16 oz. container of sour cream
2 - 8 oz. cans crescent refrigerator rolls
4 Tbsp. butter or margarine
Parmesan cheese

Brown ground beef with chopped onion and green pepper. Drain grease. Stir in: spaghetti sauce, mushrooms & olives. Place meat mixture in greased 9x13 pan. Spread sour cream over meat mixture, sprinkle with shredded mozzarella cheese. Open and unroll canned crescent rolls and place flat over cheese. Melt butter and spread over rolls. Sprinkle with parmesan cheese. Bake at 375 degrees for 20 to 30 min. or until crescent rolls are golden brown. Family favorite.

Veggies and Sausage
Marilyn Downer

1 ring smoked sausage, sliced
1 bag Green Giant veggies and cheese (broccoli, carrots, cauliflower)
Cooked rice or noodles.

Cook rice or noodles. Set aside. Cook vegetables and cheese with sliced sausage according to directions. Season to taste. Serve vegetables and sausage over rice or noodles.

Desserts

"How sweet are your words to my taste, sweeter than honey to my mouth."

Psalm 119:10

Desserts

5 Minute Chocolate Mug Cake!
Andrea V. Johnston

4 Tbsp. flour
2 Tbsp. cocoa
3 Tbsp. milk
3 Tbsp. chocolate chips
A small splash of vanilla extract
1 large coffee mug (microwave safe)

4 Tbsp. sugar
1 egg
3 Tbsp. oil

Add dry ingredients to mug and mix well. Add the egg and mix thoroughly. Pour in the milk and oil and mix well. Add the chocolate chips and vanilla extract and mix again. Put your mug in the microwave and cook for 3 min. at 1000 watts. The cake will rise over the top of the mug, but don't be alarmed! Allow to cool a little and tip out onto a plate if desired.

Angie's QUICK Pecan Pie
Angie Martin

1 Ritz pie crust or make your own
3 eggs
1 cup sugar
1/2 cup lite corn syrup
1/2 tsp. salt
1 Tbsp. flour
1 cup pecans
1 tsp. vanilla
2 Tbsp. butter

EASY....Mix well all ingredients in bowl. Pour into pie crust. Bake 1 hour at 325 degrees (Cover the last 15 minutes of baking time)

Apple Brownies
Pam Herrington

2/3 cup butter or margarine
2 eggs
1/2 cup chopped nuts (optional)
2 tsp. baking powder
2 cups brown sugar
1 tsp. vanilla
2 cups flour
1/4 tsp. salt
1 cup chopped apples (cooking apples, Macintosh, etc)

Cream butter and sugar. Add eggs and vanilla. Mix well. Add dry ingredients and mix well. Stir in apples and nuts. Bake at 350 degrees in greased 9x13 pan. Bake for 35-40 minutes or until toothpick comes out clean when inserted into the middle. Cool and then sprinkle with powdered sugar on top (optional).

Apple Crumb Pie
Beth Cowart

1 graham cracker pie crust
1 egg white, slightly beaten
1 (21 oz.) can apple pie filling
3/4 cup flour
1/4 cup sugar
1 1/2 tsp. ground cinnamon
1/4 cup margarine
3/4 cup pecans, chopped powdered sugar

Brush pie crust with egg white. Bake at 375 degrees for 5 minutes. Spoon pie filling into pie crust. In small bowl combine flour, sugar and cinnamon. Cut in the margarine until mixture is crumbly. Stir in pecans, sprinkle over pie filling. Bake for 25-30 minutes or until topping is golden brown. Serve warm and sprinkle with powdered sugar.

Apple Dumplings
Sharon Schroeter

4 Granny Smith apples
1/2 cup cinnamon/sugar
2 cup Sugar
2 tubes crescent rolls
1-1/2 cup water
1 stick butter

Peel, core & cut apples in quarters lengthwise. Separate crescent rolls & wrap each apple section, covering as much as possible. Place wrapped apples in a 9x13 pan. Sprinkle with cinnamon/sugar. Boil water, sugar & butter. Pour over apples. Sprinkle with remaining cinnamon/sugar. Bake 20-30 minutes at 350 until golden brown.

Apple Nut Cake
Lorraine Del Valle & Stacy Metz

CAKE:
1 1/2 cups oil
3 eggs
1 1/2 cups diced pecans
2 cups sugar
3 cups self-rising flour
1 tsp. vanilla
3 cups apples, diced ahead & let turn brown

TOPPING:
2 cups light brown sugar
1/2 cup evaporated milk
1 stick butter or margarine
1 tsp. vanilla

CAKE: Beat together in mixer the oil, sugar, and eggs. Add the flour and mix well. Add pecans, vanilla, and apples. Pour batter into a greased & floured tube pan. Bake at 350 for approx. 1 hour and 10 minutes.
TOPPING: Boil all ingredients on stove approx. 10 minutes (CAREFUL DON'T GET BURNED - IT WILL BE HOT). Set pot in pan of cold water and let cool. Pour over cake.

Aunt Nell's Blueberry Gook
Sandy Taylor

2 1/4 cup vanilla wafers, crushed
3/4 cup butter, melted
8 oz. cream cheese, softened
1 cup confectioners sugar
1 cup chopped nuts
1 lrg. container Cool Whip
1 can blueberry or cherry pie filling

In a 9x13 pan build layers: Layer 1: Combine vanilla wafers and melted butter and pat on bottom of pan. Layer 2: Combine cream cheese and sugar and spread on crumb mixture. Layer 3: Sprinkle on chopped nuts. Layer 4: Spread on Cool Whip. Layer 5: Spread on pie filling Refrigerate at least 2 hours, but it is best if it can be refrigerated overnight.

Baked Pineapple
Andreah Wellman

2 (#2) cans pineapple tidbits
3/4 cup sugar (or less)
3/4 - 1 stick butter
1/2 cup flour
1 stack Ritz crackers/crushed

Drain pineapple, reserving 1/4 cup juice, and spread in a greased casserole dish. Mix flour and sugar together, sprinkle over pineapple. Pour juice and stir until blended. Sprinkle crushed crackers over all. Bake at 350 for 30 minutes.

Banana Bars
Linda Rehder

1/2 cup butter or margarine (1 stick)
2 eggs well beaten
3/4 cups sour cream or buttermilk
3 mashed well ripened large bananas
1 tsp. salt

1½ cups white sugar
1 tsp. vanilla
2 cups sifted flour
1 tsp. baking soda

Frosting:
8 oz. cream cheese
1/2 cup karo white syrup
3-4 Tbsp. milk

1 cup margarine (1 stick)
4 cups powdered sugar
2 tsp. vanilla

Mix together thoroughly: butter, white sugar, eggs, sour cream or buttermilk, vanilla, bananas, flour, soda and salt. Place batter in 9x13 jelly roll pan. Bake at 350 degrees for 30-35 minutes or until toothpick comes out of center of bars clean. Cool completely. Mix together all frosting ingredients. Add more powdered sugar if needed to make thick frosting. Spread frosting over cooled bars. Should store bars in refrigerator.

Buttermilk Pie
Shea Haupt

3 eggs
1 cup buttermilk
1/4 cup flour
2 tsp. vanilla

3/4 cup sugar
1 stick butter
1 8 in unbaked pie shell

In bowl, beat eggs slightly. Add milk, melted butter, and sugar mixed with flour and vanilla. Pour in pie shell and bake at 375 for 15 minutes. Reduce heat to 300 and bake until custard is set and firm (about 30 minutes).

Banana Cream Cheesecake
Jodi Faaborg

1 pkg. (2-layer size) white cake mix, divided
4 eggs, divided
2/3 cup packed brown sugar, divided
2 Tbsp. lemon juice
3 Tbsp. oil
2 bananas, sliced
1 1/2 cups milk
2 pkg. (8 oz.. each) Philadelphia cream cheese, softened
1 1/2 cups thawed Cool Whip whipped topping

Heat oven to 300 degrees. Reserve 1 cup dry cake mix. Mix remaining cake mix with 1 egg, oil and 1/3 cup sugar with mixer. (Mixture will be crumbly.) Press onto bottom and 1 inch up sides of greased 13x9 inch baking pan; top with bananas. Beat cream cheese and remaining sugar with mixture. Add reserved cake mix, remaining eggs and lemon juice; beat 1 minute. Blend in milk. (Batter will be very thin.) Pour into crust. Bake 45 to 50 minutes or until center is almost set. Cool. Refrigerate 4 hours. Top with Cool Whip. Refrigerate leftovers. Note: Wrap leftovers in foil. Freeze. When ready to serve, thaw in refrigerator.

Berry Freeze
Pam Herrington

1 can (14 oz.) sweetened condensed milk
¼ cup lemon juice
2 cups mini marshmallows
1/2 cup chopped pecans
1 can (16 oz.) whole berry cranberry sauce
1 (8 oz.) whipped topping, thawed
1 (20 oz.) can crushed pineapple, drained

In large bowl whip together sweetened condensed milk and lemon juice. Stir in marshmallow, cranberry sauce, crushed pineapple and pecans. Fold in thawed topping. Put in 13x9x 2 dish. Freeze until firm or you can make the day before. Cut in squares and serve.

Banana Pudding
Angie Martin

2 cup sugar (less, sweeten to your liking)
3/4 cup self rising flour
dash of salt
4 cups milk
1 Tbsp. vanilla
6 egg yolks (keep whites for meringue)
3 to 4 bananas
2 boxes NABISCO vanilla wafers (use 1 1/2 boxes in layers save the rest for decoration)
1/4 tsp. cream of tartar

Custard... Combine flour and sugar. Mix well in medium size pot. Add milk, eggs and vanilla. Stir continually, slowly on medium heat approx 20 minutes until almost thick (longer you stir over medium heat thicker custard gets) Let sit. Quickly layer bananas and vanilla wafers in casserole dish (thin or deep dish looks best in clear dish) Pour custard mixture over and down into layers. **Meringue**... Beat egg whites on low speed 3 to 4 minutes to get air in them. Then add cold water slowly by the teaspoon while beating (about 2 tsp). Beat 1 minute. Add 1/4 cream of tarter. Beat 1 to 2 minutes. Add 1 to 2 vanilla (clear if you have it) and approx 4 tsp of sugar. Beat until fluffy. Add to top of custard and layered bananas and cookies. Decorate edge of dish with left over vanilla wafers. Broil to brown top of meringue to light to medium brown. (DO NOT CLOSE OVEN DOOR WHILE BROWNING MERINGUE) Serve warm or cold.

Brian's Favorite-Hoosier Sugar Cream Pie
Betsy Hall

1 1/3 cups sugar
1/2 cup all purpose flour, unsifted
1/2 pint (1 cup) whipping cream
3/4 cup milk
1 (9 in.) unbaked pie shell (I make my own)
2 Tbsp. butter, cut into small pieces
Pinch nutmeg (I omit)

Preheat oven to 450. Combine sugar, flour, cream, and milk in a mixing bowl. Pour into pie shell. Dot with butter bits all around the top of pie. Sprinkle with nutmeg, if desired. Bake for approximately 10 minutes, and then reduce the heat to 350 degrees and cook for approx. 30 more minutes. Cool to room temperature and then refrigerate until chilled. Serve chilled. (Should be a light golden brown on top...may need an extra min. or two.) Enjoy this Hoosier tradition! Go Indiana!

Carolina Chewy Bars
Sharon Willis (In Memory of Pam Willis)

1/2 cup butter, softened
3 eggs
1 tsp. vanilla
Powdered sugar

1 lb. light brown sugar
2 cup self rising flour
1 cup chopped pecans

Cream butter and sugar. Add eggs, beating well. Blend in flour. Stir in remaining ingredients (except powered sugar). Spread batter into a well greased and lightly floured 13x9x2 inch pan. Bake at 300 for 45 minutes to an hour. Cool, dust with powered sugar and cut into bars.

Best-Ever Chocolate Fudge Layer Cake
Holly McAndrew

1 pkg. (8 squares) Baker's semi-sweet baking chocolate, divided
1 pkg. chocolate cake mix (w/out pudding)
1 pkg. (4-serving size) Jell-o Chocolate flavor instant pudding
4 eggs
1 cup Breakstone's or Knudsen sour cream
1/2 cup oil
1/2 cup water
1 tub (8 oz.) frozen Cool Whip topping
2 Tbsp. Planters sliced almonds

Preheat oven to 350. Grease 2-9" round baking pans. Chop 2 of the chocolate squares; set aside. Beat cake mix, dry pudding mix, eggs, sour cream, oil and water in large bowl with electric mixer on low speed just until moistened. Beat on medium speed 2 min. Stir in chopped chocolate. Spoon into prepared pans. Bake 30-35 min. or until wooden toothpick inserted in centers comes out clean. Cool in pans on wire racks. 10 min. Loosen cakes from sides of pans. Invert onto racks; gently remove pans. Cool cakes completely. Place frozen whipped topping and remaining 6 chocolate squares in the microwaveable bowl. Microwave on HIGH for 1 1/2 min. or until chocolate is completely melted and mixture is smooth, stirring after 1 min. Let stand 15 min. to thicken. Place 1 cake layer on serving plate; top with 1/4 of the chocolate mixture and the second cake layer. Spread top and side with remaining chocolate mixture. Garnish with almonds. Store in refrigerator. Servings: 18

Bruleed Banana Splits
Dave Friss

2 Bananas
Vanilla Ice Cream
Cooking Torch

Granulated sugar
Caramel Sauce

Flip a baking sheet upside down on the counter, and cover with several sheets of heavy duty aluminum foil (creates an air space so you don't burn your counter). Quarter the unpeeled bananas. Fill the bottom of a bowl with the sugar, and press the cut side of the bananas into the sugar to coat. Place the sugared bananas on the foil cooking rig. Sprinkle with more sugar. Follow the manufacturer's instructions to ignite and operate the cooking torch. Apply the small blue triangle of flame nearest the tip of the torch to the first banana, using constant motion. The sugar should melt, then turn brown. Work the flame up and down the banana not leaving any sugar uncooked. Make sure to use constant motion so the fruit doesn't burn. Allow to cool for a few seconds, and then tapping lightly with a metal spoon to ensure that a crunch candy shell has been created. Repeat with the remaining bananas.

Drizzle a bit of caramel sauce on the bottom of the bowl in a zig zag pattern. Place four banana pieces in the bowl leaving a bit of space in the middle. Put a scoop of vanilla ice cream in the center of the bananas. Drizzle with more caramel sauce.

Makes two banana splits.

Carrot Cake
Pam Herrington

2 cups sugar	2 cups flour
2 tsp. cinnamon	2 tsp. soda
1 tsp. salt	1 cup oil
4 eggs	3 cups raw, grated carrots

Sift and mix dry ingredients. Add oil and stir well. Add eggs, one at a time, and stir well after each addition. Add carrots and blend thoroughly. Place in two 9 inch pans or 1 loaf cake pan which have been greased and floured. Bake at 350 for 45 min or until toothpick comes out clean.

Cherry Chocolate Bars
Hilary Bertke

32 Hershey kisses
2 egg, slightly beaten
1 box Devil's food cake mix with pudding
21 oz. can of cherry pie filling
1 Tbsp. of almond extract

Unwrap kisses. Set aside. Heat oven to 350. Grease and flour 15x10x1 jelly roll pan. In large bowl beat eggs, add extract, and pie filling. Mix well. Add cake mix and blend. Spread batter in pan. Bake 28-30 min. Immediately remove from oven. Lightly score baked dough into 32 bars. Put a kiss on each bar. Refrigerate until cool. Cover.

Carrot Cake
Sue Powell

Cake:
1-3/4 cup sugar   1-1/4 cup vegetable oil
4 unbeaten eggs   2 cup flour
1 tsp. salt   3 cup grated carrots
2 tsp. each baking soda, baking powder and cinnamon

Frosting:
1 small can crushed pineapple, drained
1 stick butter, room temperature
1 8 oz. cream cheese, room temperature
2 Tbsp. vanilla
1 box confectioner's sugar

Grease and flour 3-9" round cake pans. **Cake**: Blend with mixer the first three ingredients, adding eggs one at a time. Mix together flour, salt, baking soda, baking powder and cinnamon and add to mixture. Fold in carrots. Divide evenly in three pans. Bake at 350 for 25-35 minutes. Let cool for a few minutes and then remove from pans and continue to cool. **Filling & Frosting**: Drain pineapple. Cream butter, cream cheese, and vanilla. Add confectioner's sugar a little at a time. Take 1/4 of frosting and mix with pineapple. This mixture goes between the layers of the cake. Frost the rest of cake with remaining frosting. Refrigerate cake. Can be removed a few minutes before serving, but needs to be stored in refrigerator.

Carrot Cake
Linda Jesel

Cake:
2 cup plain flour	2 cup sugar
2 tsp. baking soda	2 tsp. cinnamon
1 tsp. salt	1 1/2 cup vegetable oil
4 eggs	3 cup grated carrots

1/2 to 3/4 cup each: Pineapple and Raisins
1 cup chopped walnuts or pecans
Optional: 1/2 tsp. each of ground cloves and nutmeg.

Icing:
1 large package of cream cheese
1 stick butter or margarine
1 box confectioner's sugar
2 tsp. vanilla
1 cup chopped pecans

Cake:
Sift and mix dried ingredients. Add oil and stir well. Add eggs, one at a time and mix after each. Add carrots, pineapple and raisins, mixing after each. Pour into two floured 9 or 10 inch cake pans. Bake at 350 degrees for about 25 minutes. Don't be surprised if the cake takes longer. Pineapple and raisins can make it take longer. Test for doneness: insert toothpick or turkey lacer into the center. If it comes out clean, cake should be done. You can also try the light press method. If cake springs back, even slowly, it should be done.

Icing:
Cream together the butter and cream cheese. Add sugar and vanilla, mix in thoroughly. Be sure the cake is cool enough to frost. Apply the icing, then sprinkle the nuts over the icing as decoration. Enjoy!

Cheese Cake
Lynn Francisco for Greer Mimbs

Crust:
3/4 cup Graham Cracker Crumbs
1 Tbsp. sugar
1 Tbsp. melted butter (or more)
 Filling :
3 packs 8 oz. cream cheese, softened
4 eggs
1 tsp. vanilla
1 cup sugar
Topping:
2 cup sour cream
1 Tbsp. sugar
1 tsp. vanilla

Crust - Mix together - pat in 9 inch spring form pan. Refrigerate while making filling.
Filling - Beat cream cheese until fluffy and add all other ingredients and beat until fluffy. Pour onto crust. Bake at 375 degrees for 35 minutes.
Topping- Mix together spread over cheesecake. Re-bake for 5 minutes. Cool in pan. Do no put in fridge until completely cooled.

Chess Bars
Brenda Bakos

Bottom layer:
1 box yellow cake mix
1 egg, well beaten
1 stick butter, melted

Top layer:
8 oz. cream cheese
1 box (16 oz.) confectioner's sugar
2 eggs, well beaten

Mix bottom layer ingredients together and press into a greased 9x13 inch pan. Combine all the ingredients for the top layer, and beat with mixer until smooth. Pour this over the top of the first layer, and evenly distribute. Bake for 35-40 minutes or until golden brown in the oven at 350 degrees. When cool, cut into squares and serve. Yummy!!!

Chocolate Lover's Cake
Rae Sprow

1 box dark chocolate cake mix
1 small box instant chocolate pudding mix
1 (16 oz.) container sour cream
3 eggs
1/3 cup vegetable oil
1/2 cup coffee flavored liqueur like Kahlua
2 cups semi-sweet chocolate chips

Preheat oven to 350 degrees. Grease and flour a 10-inch bundt pan. In a large bowl, combine cake mix, pudding mix, sour cream, eggs, oil and coffee liqueur. Beat until ingredients are well blended. Fold in chocolate chips. Batter will be thick. Spoon into prepared pan. Bake in oven for 1 hour, or until cake springs back when lightly tapped. Cool 10 minutes in pan, then turn out and cool completely on wire rack.

Chocolate-Dipped Macaroons
Aileen Freeman

14 oz. can sweetened condensed milk
14 oz. sweetened, flaked coconut
1 Tbsp. grated orange peel
1 tsp. vanilla
Whites from 2 large eggs
12 oz. bag semi-sweet chocolate chips

Combine milk, coconut, orange peel and vanilla in large bowl. Line a baking sheet with foil; spray foil with Pam. Dust with flour, or use Baker's Joy. Beat egg whites with mixer in a small-medium bowl until stiff peaks form when mixer is lifted. Fold into coconut mixture. Use a level tablespoon to make the cookies and put onto baking sheet. Bake 14-16 minutes at 325 degrees until lightly toasted. Lift foil out of pan and place over a wire rack to cool the cookies. After the cookies are totally done, remove the foil from the cookies. Keep foil. Melt chocolate chips. Dip bottoms of macaroons in chocolate and put cookies back onto the foil. Slide foil back onto baking sheets. Refrigerate until chocolate sets. Peel off foil. Store in refrigerator in tightly closed container. Put waxed paper between layers of cookies. Yummy!

Chocolate Pretzel Rings
Pam Herrington

48-50 pretzel rings or mini twists
1 pkg. (8 oz.) chocolate kisses
1/4 cup M&M's

Place the pretzels on greased cooking sheets. Place a chocolate kiss in the center of each ring. Bake a 275 for 2-3 minutes or until chocolate is softened. Remove from oven. Place an M&M on each, pressing down slightly so chocolate fills ring. Refrigerate for 5-10 min or until chocolate is firm. Stir in airtight container at room temperature.
Yield: Approx 4 dozen

Chocolate-Raspberry Brownies
Pam Herrington

1 cup unsalted butter, softened
5 squares unsweetened baking chocolate, chopped
2 cups sugar
4 eggs
2 tsp. vanilla extract
1 1/4 cup all purpose flour
1 tsp. baking powder
1/2 tsp. salt
1 cup chopped walnuts, toasted (optional)
1/2 cup raspberry preserves

Melt butter and chocolate in heavy saucepan over low heat, stirring constantly until smooth. Remove from heat. Whisk in sugar, eggs and vanilla. Mix flour, baking powder and salt in a small bowl. Add to chocolate mixture and whisk to blend. Stir in nuts. Pour 2 cups batter into the bottom of a greased 9 x 2 pan. Freeze until firm, about 10 minutes. Spread preserves over frozen brownie batter in pan, spoon remaining batter over preserves. Let stand for 20 minutes at room temperature to thaw. Bake brownies at 350 degrees for approx. 35 minutes, or until tester comes out clean. Transfer to rack to cool. Makes about 2 dozen brownies

Chocolate Coconut Drums
Claudia Mathis

2 cups shredded coconut
3 Tbsp. condensed milk
1 cup cooking chocolate, shredded

Place coconut and milk in a mixing bowl. Mix until a paste is formed. Form the coconut paste into small balls and flatten with fingers. Allow 1 hour to dry. Melt the chocolate and dip the coconut shapes until fully covered. Place on wax paper to dry.

Chocolate Revel Bars
Linda Rehder

1 cup butter or margarine (2 sticks)
2 cup brown sugar
1 tsp. salt
2 ½ cups flour

2 eggs
1 tsp. baking soda
2 tsp. vanilla
3 cups quick oatmeal

Filling:
12 oz. pkg. of semi-sweet chocolate chips
15 oz. can sweetened condensed milk
2 Tbsp. butter or margarine
1/2 tsp. salt
1 cup chopped walnuts (optional)
2 tsp. vanilla

In mixing bowl cream butter, brown sugar and eggs. Beat well. Add: baking soda, eggs, salt, vanilla and flour. Beat well. Last add oatmeal and beat until well mixed. Spread ¾ of mixture in well greased 9x13 jelly roll pan. (Reserving ¼ of mixture for topping). In double boiler place: chocolate chip, sweetened condensed milk, butter and salt. Stir until chocolate chips are completely melted. Then add nuts and vanilla. Spread this filling over batter already in jelly roll pan. In small amounts, dot remaining batter over filling. Bake at 350 degrees, 15-20 minutes or until golden in color. Let cool completely before cutting.

Church Windows
Liz Collins

1 stick butter or margarine
12 oz. chocolate chips
1 cup chopped nuts
1 pkg. small colored marshmallows
1 cup shredded coconut

In 2 1/2 qt. pot melt butter & chocolate over low heat -- remove --cool slightly. Add nuts & marshmallows. Stir until coated. Shape into two logs. Coat with coconut or nuts. Refrigerate & slice. Keep refrigerated.

Crockpot Candy
Jannon Pierce

16 oz. unsalted dry peanuts
1 German chocolate bar
12 oz. pkg. chocolate chips
1 1/2 pkg. white chocolate (Almond Bark)
16 oz. salted dry peanuts
1/3 pkg. peanut butter chips

Place all ingredients in crock pot. Turn on low and cook for 2 hours and 15 minutes. DO NOT LIFT LID! Stir thoroughly. Drop on wax paper by teaspoon. Makes 100-150 pieces.

Citrus Streusel Quick Bread
Nancy Brining

1 package (18-1/4 ounces) lemon or orange cake mix, divided
2 Tbsp. brown sugar
1 tsp. ground cinnamon
1 Tbsp. cold butter or margarine
1/2 cup chopped pecans or walnuts
1 pkg. instant vanilla pudding mix (if you can find it orange instant pudding mix works well too)
4 eggs (can use egg substitute)
1 cup (8 oz.) sour cream
1/3 cup vegetable oil

GLAZE:
1 cup confectioner's sugar   2-3 Tbsp. cold milk

In a small bowl, combine 2Tbsp cake mix, brown sugar, and cinnamon; cut in the butter until crumbly. Stir in pecans; set aside. In a mixing bowl, combine the pudding mix, eggs, sour cream, oil and remaining cake mix. Beat on medium speed. Pour into two greased 8x2 inch loaf pans. Sprinkle with pecan mixture. Bake at 350 for 45 to 50 minutes or until a toothpick inserted in the center comes out clean. Cool in pans ten minutes before removing to cooling racks. Combine glaze ingredients; drizzle over warm bread. Yields: 2 loaves. This was my father's recipe (Clifford Wilcox) and I'm submitting it in his memory, at the end he left a comment "You better make several at a time". This is a good idea because it's so good and it doesn't last long once it comes out of the oven.

Creamy Cheese 'N Cherry Pie
Susan Bassler

3 cups Kelloggs Rice Krispies cereal
1/4 cup sugar
1 8oz. container sour cream
4 pkgs. cream cheese, softened
1 tsp. vanilla
2 tsp. lemon juice
1 can cherry pie filling or blueberry
1/2 cup butter
1/2 tsp. cinnamon
2 Tbsp. sugar
2 eggs
1/3 cup sugar

Crush cereal to 1 1/2 cups and set aside. Melt butter in a small saucepan over low heat. Remove from heat and stir in 1/4 cup sugar and cinnamon, and add crushed cereal. Mix well. With back of spoon press mixture evenly and firmly around bottom and sides of a 9-inch pie pan to form crust. Set aside. In a small mixing bowl, mix together sour cream and 2 Tbsp of sugar. Set aside. In a large mixing bowl, beat cream cheese until smooth. Add eggs, vanilla, 1/3 cup sugar, and 1 tsp of lemon juice. Beat until mixed well. Pour mixture into cereal crust and bake in oven at 375 for about 20 minutes or until set. Remove from oven and spread sour cream mixture over top. Return to oven. Bake 5 minutes longer, remove from oven and cool. In small mixing bowl, mix pie filing with the remaining 1 tsp lemon juice. Spread over top of cooked pie. Refrigerate until thoroughly chilled.

The Easiest Fudge
Sheila Mathis

1 12 oz. bag milk chocolate chips
1 16 oz. can ready-to-spread milk chocolate frosting

Lightly butter an 8 or 9 inch square baker pan. In non-stick pan over low heat, melt chocolate chips and frosting, stirring frequently until smooth. Pour fudge into prepared baker. Cool in refrigerator. You can also use peanut butter chips and vanilla frosting for peanut butter fudge.

Danish Apple Pastry Bars
Linda Rehder

2 ½ cups flour
1 cup Crisco, solid shortening
1 cup sugar
3 Tbsp. flour
1 cup crushed cornflakes

1 tsp. salt
8 large or 10 medium cooking apples
2 tsp. cinnamon
1 egg, separated

Frosting: 1 cup powdered sugar, 2-3 Tbsp. milk

Place Crisco (solid shortening) in mixing bowl. Cut in with a pastry cutter 2 1/2 cups flour and salt. Place 1 beaten egg yolk in measuring cup, add enough milk to egg yolk to equal 2/3 cup. Add milk mixture to flour mixture. Mix with pastry cutter. Divide dough into 2 balls. Roll out first ball onto a floured surface. Roll to cover bottom of a 9x13 jelly roll pan, let crust fall slightly over edges of pan. Do not trim crust edges. Sprinkle crust with crushed cornflakes. Peel and slice apples and spread over corn flakes in pan. In bowl mix: sugar, cinnamon and 3 Tbsp of flour. Stir until well mixed, and then sprinkle over apples. Roll out second ball of pastry dough large enough to over apple mixture in pan. Place rolled out dough on apples and seal edges of bottom layer of dough with the top layer. Slightly beat egg white and brush over top layer of pastry dough. Make several cuts in top of dough like you would an apple pie. Bake at 400 degrees, 1 hour. If crust is browning too quickly before apples are cooked, tent with aluminum foil to protect. Let bars cool to slightly warm or cool then mix powdered sugar and milk in bowl and drizzle over bars.

Easy Oatmeal Cookie
Brenda Bakos

3/4 cup butter
1/2 cup white sugar
3 cups oatmeal
1/4 cup water
1 cup all-purpose flour
1 cup firmly packed brown sugar
1/2 tsp. baking soda
1 egg
1 tsp. cinnamon
1 tsp. salt

Mix ingredients together, and bake at 350 degrees for 8-9 minutes.

Easy Peanut Butter Cookies
Megan Johnson

1 box Jiffy white cake mix
1/3 cup sugar
Extra sugar (optional)
1 cup peanut butter
3 Tbsp. water

Preheat oven to 350 degrees. Mix cake mix, peanut butter, sugar and water. Roll dough into small balls. Place on ungreased cookie sheet about an inch apart. Flatten with a fork (one vertical press/one horizontal press) sprinkle lightly with extra sugar (if desired) Bake in the oven for about 10 min. or until golden on bottom. Let cool.

Fabulous Cheesecake
Keith Martin

Filling:
3 (8 oz.) cream cheese   4 eggs
1 1/2 cup sugar
Crust:
52 vanilla wafers (crushed)   1 stick margarine
Topping:
8 oz. sour cream   1/2 cup sugar

Crust - Crush vanilla wafers, pour into spring form pan. Melt margarine and pour over wafers. Pat into bottom of pan.

Filling - Mix all ingredients together well and pour over crust. Bake in 350 oven for 45 min.

Topping - Mix sour cream and sugar together & pour over cake. Continue baking for 15 minutes longer.

Fantastic Fudge
Brenda Bakos

5 cups granulated sugar
1 large (12oz.) can evaporated milk
2 sticks butter or margarine
2 - 12 oz. packages chocolate chips
1 large jar marshmallow cream
1 tsp. vanilla
2 cups chopped nuts (pecans, English walnuts, etc.)

Combine sugar, milk, and butter in a large heavy saucepan. Bring to a boil over medium heat stirring constantly. Cook to soft ball (240 degrees) stage on a candy thermometer or about 9 minutes. Remove from heat, and fold in chocolate chips well. Stir in vanilla and marshmallow cream; then add nuts. Pour into buttered 9x13 pan and cool in refrigerator until firm. Cut into squares and enjoy! This fudge stays fresh in a tightly sealed container for about a month.

Flourless Chocolate Cake
Jean McIntyre

6 ounces bittersweet chocolate (at least 60% cocoa like Ghirardelli)
6 Tbsp. butter or margarine
3/4 cup sugar in the raw
4 eggs, separated
Pinch of salt

Preheat oven to 300. Line the bottom of an 8 inch pan with parchment paper. In a double boiler, melt chocolate and butter. Beat egg whites with a pinch of salt until stiff peaks form. Once the chocolate and butter are thoroughly melted, take off stove. Add sugar and egg yolks. Fold in the beaten egg whites. Pour into 8 inch pan, and bake for 40-50 minutes. Top will crack slightly when done. Take out of oven and let cool for 20 minutes before removing from pan. Cake will shrink to about half its height. Dust with powdered sugar before serving.

Gooey Dessert Bars
Katrina West

1 box yellow cake mix
1 cup firmly packed brown sugar
1/2 cup butter (1 stick), softened
2 large eggs, lightly beaten
2 tsp. vanilla extract
1 (6 oz.) semi-sweet chocolate chips

Preheat oven to 350 degrees. In the large bowl of an electric mixer, combine cake mix, brown sugar, butter, eggs and vanilla. Mix on medium speed until well blended. Pour into a greased 9 x 13 baking dish. Sprinkle chocolate chips on top. Bake for 30 minutes. Do not over bake, even though bars may not appear to be done. Cool and cut into bars.

Flourless Peanut Butter Cookies
Pam Herrington

2 cups creamy peanut butter
2 cups packed light brown sugar
2 large eggs
2 tsp. baking soda
1 cup coarsely, chopped cocktail peanuts
1/2 cup heavy cream
1 cup bittersweet chocolate chips
Chopped peanuts

Heat oven to 350. Cookies: Beat peanut butter, sugar, eggs and baking soda in large bowl with eclectic mixer 2 min or until smooth and blended. Stir in chopped peanuts Drop level Tbsp. full of dough 2 in apart on ungreased baking sheets Bake, one sheet at a time, for 10 min or until cookies are puffed and slightly golden. Cool 5 min on baking sheet, remove to wire racks to cool completely Ganache: Microwave cream in glass bowl on high for one min or until it begins to simmer Add chocolate chips - let stand 2 min Stir until chocolate is melted and smooth Spread over half of cookie top and sprinkle with chopped peanuts. If remaining ganache begins to firm up microwave a few seconds at a time until easy to spread Let set at room temperature

Fruit and Nut Cookies
Larry Wise

Combine in large bowl the following ingredients:
2 cups whole pitted dates
2 cups whole candied cherries (1 cup red, 1 cup green) I have also used dried cherries and cranberries, drained maraschino cherries, fruit cake mix)
2 cups whole candied pineapple
2 cups whole pecans (I used chopped)
2 cups whole English walnuts (I used chopped)
2 cups Brazil nuts (I used sliced almonds)
Cream together:
1 lb. soft butter with 1 cup brown sugar   1 cup white sugar
1 tsp. vanilla   1 tsp. salt
1 tsp. soda

Beat in 3 eggs, one at a time. Add 5 cup flour. Add the fruits and nuts and mix well. (I use my hands to mix in the fruit.) Roll like jelly roll on wax paper, makes 4 large jelly rolls. Then wrap in foil and seal tight. Put in plastic bags and freeze. Defrost slightly, slice with sharp knife about 1/4 inch thick. Sprinkle with sugar. Bake at 350 for 8-10 minutes. Keeps up to 6 months.

Gooey Pecan Bars
Janice Sprowles

1 (18 oz.) pkg. butter pecan cake mix
1 8 oz. pkg. cream cheese, softened
1 16 oz. pkg. powdered sugar, sifted
1 cup butter or margarine, melted and divided
1 egg, lightly beaten
2 eggs
1 1/2 cups chopped pecans

Preheat oven to 350 degrees. Combine cake mix, 1 egg and 1/2 cup butter. Press into bottom of a lightly greased 13 x 9 x 2 inch pan. Set aside. Combine 2 eggs, cream cheese, powdered sugar and remaining 1/2 cup butter; beat at medium speed with an electric mixer until smooth. Stir in pecans and pour over cake mix layer. Bake at 350 for 50 minutes or until set. Covering loosely with aluminum foil after 45 minutes. Cool on a wire rack. Cut into squares.

Grandma Del Valle Cookies
Lorraine Del Valle & Stacy Metz

1/2 cup butter or shortening
1 egg
2-3 Tbsp. milk
1/2 tsp. baking powder
1/2 tsp. salt
1/2 tsp. grated orange peel (1 tsp. orange extract can be substituted)
1 cup sugar
1/2 tsp. vanilla
2 cups plain flour
1/2 tsp. baking soda

In mixer cream shortening & sugar well. Add egg and beat well. Add vanilla & orange peel and mix well. Sift all dry ingredients and alternately add with milk - mix well. Drop onto greased cookie sheet with heaping Tbsp. Decorate with colored sugar, raisins, nuts, frosting, etc. Bake at 375 degrees for approx. 9 - 12 minutes.

Georgia Style Chocolate Cake
Carla Kelly

2 cups flour
1/2 tsp. salt
1 stick butter
3/4 cup vegetable oil
1/2 cup buttermilk
2 eggs

2 cups sugar
1 cup water
3 Tbsp. cocoa
1 tsp. soda
1 tsp. vanilla

Frosting:
1 stick butter 1 (16 oz.) confectioner's sugar
1 Tbsp. cocoa
6 Tbsp. evaporated milk
2 tsp. vanilla
1 cup chopped pecans

Combine in 2 qt. pan, bring to simmer. Do NOT boil. Pour over cake when cool.

Cake:
Combine flour, sugar and salt in large bowl; set aside. Mix water, butter, cocoa and vegetable oil in 2 quart saucepan. Bring to boil and add to flour mixture. Combine soda, buttermilk and vanilla. Put into flour mixture. Add eggs, beating well after each addition. Pour into 11x16 cookie sheet with sides. Bake 20 min. Frost with above frosting.

Holiday Pumpkin/Mincemeat Treats
Marge Wise

1 3/4 cups flour
1/3 cup firmly packed brown sugar
1 cup (2 sticks) cold butter
1 (15 oz.) can pumpkin (2 cups)
1/2 tsp. ground allspice
1 (27 oz.) jar None Such Ready-to-Use Mincemeat
1 (14 oz.) can Eagle Brand sweetened condensed milk (not evap. milk)
1/3 cup sugar
2 eggs
1 cup chopped nuts
1 tsp. ground cinnamon
1/2 tsp. salt

Preheat oven to 425. Combine flour and sugars. Cut in butter until crumbly. Stir in nuts. Reserving 1 1/2 cups crumb mixture. Press remaining crumb mixture on bottom and halfway up the sides of 9x13 baking dish. Spoon None Such mincemeat over crust. Combine remaining ingredients except reserved crumb mixture. Mix well. Pour over None Such. Top with reserved crumb mixture. Bake 15 minutes, reduce oven to 350. Bake 40 minutes longer or until golden brown around edges. Cool. Cut into squares. Serve warm or at room temperature. Store leftovers covered in refrigerator. Prep time 20 minutes. Makes 10-12 bars

Honey Bun Cake
Heather Boswell

1 box yellow cake mix
8 oz. sour cream
1 cup brown sugar
1/2 cup powdered sugar
1/2 cup milk
4 eggs
2/3 cup vegetable oil
1 Tbsp. cinnamon
1 tsp. vanilla

Combine cake mix, eggs, sour cream, and vegetable oil. Mix together and pour half in a 9x13 baking pan. Mix brown sugar and cinnamon. Sprinkle over half of batter in pan. Pour rest of batter over brown sugar mixture. Bake at 350 for 30-35 min.

TOPPING: combine powdered sugar, vanilla, milk. While cake is warm poke holes in cake with toothpick. Pour over cake.

Jello Custard
Claudia Mathis

4 boxes of lemon jello
1 can evaporated milk
1 8 oz. cream cheese bar
4 cups water
1 can condensed milk
1 can pineapple bits

Bring water to a boil and add the jello. Blend the evaporated, condensed milk, and the cream cheese until smooth. Blend all ingredients together. Let jello cool for about 3 hours. Decorate with pineapple bits on top

Italian Cream Cake
Janice Sprowles

Cake:
1 stick margarine
2 cup sugar
2 cups all purpose flour
1 cup buttermilk
1 small can flaked coconut
5 egg whites, stiffly beaten
1/2 cup vegetable shortening
5 egg yolks
1 tsp. baking soda
1 tsp. vanilla
1/2 cup chopped pecans

Frosting:
1 8 oz. pkg. cream cheese
1 lb. box powdered sugar
1/2 cup chopped pecans
1/2 stick butter
1 tsp. vanilla
1/2 cup coconut

Cake: Cream margarine and vegetable shortening, add sugar, and beat until mixture is smooth. Add egg yolks, beat well. Sift flour with baking soda. Add flour alternately with buttermilk to the creamed mixture. Stir in vanilla, coconut and pecans. Fold in egg whites. Pour batter into 3 greased and floured 8 inch cake pans. Bake at 350 degrees for 25 minutes. When cake is thoroughly cool, frost with cream cheese frosting. **Frosting:** Beat cream cheese and butter until creamy. Gradually add powdered sugar, mix well. Add vanilla. Assemble cake, spread frosting between layers and over top and sides of cake. Sprinkle chopped pecans and coconut on top.

Kentucky Derby Pie
Samantha Slade

1/2 cup flour
1 cup walnuts
2 eggs lightly beaten
1 tsp. vanilla

1 cup sugar
1 cup chocolate chips
1 stick butter, melted
1 pie crust

Preheat oven to 325 degrees. Combine sugar and flour. Add melted butter, eggs and vanilla to flour mixture and mix until well blended and smooth. Stir in walnuts and chocolate chips. Spread into a deep dish unbaked pie shell. Bake at 325 degrees for 45 minutes. Cool and serve warm with a dollop of whipped cream or a small scoop of ice cream.

Jewish Jimmy Coffee Cake
Becky Wessel

1 yellow cake mix
1 cup strong coffee
4 eggs

1 pkg. vanilla instant pudding
1/2 cup oil
1/4 cup chocolate Jimmies

Topping:
1/4 cup chocolate Jimmies
1 Tbsp. white sugar

1 Tbsp. brown sugar

Preheat oven to 360 degrees. Grease and flour bottom of angel food cake pan. Mix cake ingredients (cake mix, pudding, coffee, oil, and eggs) for 4 minutes. Fold in Jimmies. Pour batter into pan and sprinkle on topping. Bake for 40 minutes or until cake tester comes out clean.

Key Lime Cake
Heather Boswell

1 pkg. lemon cake without pudding
1 3/4 oz. instant lemon pudding
4 eggs
1 cup water, minus 1 - 2 Tbsp.
 Key lime juice
1 cup Wesson oil

Topping:
2 cup confectioner's sugar   1/3 cup key lime juice

Mix all ingredients together. Grease and flour 13x9 pan. Bake at 325 for 45-55 min. Let cool then poke the top with a fork. Pour topping over top (ingredients above).

Kim's Chocolate Cherry Cake
Kim Barger

2 cups flour   3/4 cup sugar
1 tsp. baking soda   1 teaspoon cinnamon
1/8 tsp. salt   2 eggs, beaten
1/2 cup canola or vegetable oil   2 tsp. vanilla
1 - 21 oz. canned cherry pie filling 1 cup chocolate chips
1 cup chopped walnuts   Powdered sugar

In large bowl, mix flour, sugar, soda, cinnamon and salt. In another bowl, mix eggs, oil and vanilla; add to flour mixture. Mix well. Stir in cherry pie filling, chocolate pieces and nuts. Pour cherry mixture into a greased and floured Bundt pan. Bake at 350 degrees for 1 hour. Cool in pan for 15 minutes. Remove from pan and cool. Sift powdered sugar on top of cake.

Key Lime Pie
Samantha Slade

For crust:
1 1/4 graham cracker crumbs
2 Tbsp. sugar
5 Tbsp. unsalted butter, melted

For filling:
1 (14 oz.) can sweetened condensed milk
4 large egg yolks
1/2 cup plus 2 Tbsp. fresh or bottled key lime juice
3/4 cup chilled heavy cream

Preheat oven to 350 degrees Stir together graham cracker crumbs, sugar, and butter in a bowl with a fork until combined well. Press mixture evenly onto bottom and up side of a 9-inch glass pie plate. Bake crust in middle of oven 10 minutes and cool on a rack. Leave oven on. Whisk together condensed milk and egg yolks in a bowl until combined well. Add lime juice and whisk until combined well (mixture will thicken slightly) Pour filling into crust and bake in middle of oven for 15 minutes. Cool pie completely on rack (filling will set as it cools), then chill, covered, at least 4 hours. Make topping just before serving, beat cream in a bowl with an electric mixer until stiff peaks form. Serve pie topped with whipped cream.

Layered Banana Pineapple Dessert
Gertrude Garland

1 1/2 cups graham cracker crumbs
1/3 cup margarine or butter, melted
1 8 oz. pkg. cream cheese, softened
2 pkgs. (4-serving size) vanilla instant pudding
1 can (20 oz.) crushed pineapple, drained
1 tub (8 oz.) cool whip, thawed
1/4 cup sugar
3 bananas, sliced
3 1/2 cups cold milk

Mix graham crackers crumbs, sugar and margarine in 9x13 inch pan. Press evenly onto bottom of pan. Arrange banana slices on crust. Beat cream cheese in large bowl with wire whisk until smooth. Gradually beat in milk. Add pudding mixes. Beat until well blended. Spread evenly over banana slices. Spoon pineapple evenly over pudding mixture. Spread whipped topping over pineapple. Refrigerate 3 hours or until ready to serve. Makes 15 servings.

Lemon Bars
Linda Rehder

Crust:
3 cups flour
1 ½ cups butter or margarine (3 sticks)
3/4 cup powdered sugar

Filling:
6 eggs, beaten
3 cups white sugar
1 tsp. baking powder
1/2 cups fresh lemon juice
1/2 cups flour

Topping: 1/4 cup powdered sugar

Place 3/4 powdered sugar and 3 cups flour into mixing bowl cut margarine into mixture, then softly knead together into a ball. Press mixture into bottom of 9x13 jelly roll pan. Mix the following together for filling: eggs, lemon juice, white sugar, and 1/2 cup flour and baking powder. Mix well and pour over crust already in pan. Bake at 350 degrees for 25-35 minutes until filling is set up. Sift 1/4 cup powdered sugar over cooled bars.

Lemon Bars
Marilyn Downer

2 cups flour
2/3 cup and 1 Tbsp. powdered sugar
1 cup butter
8 large eggs
1 1/2 cups sugar
1 cup bottled lemon juice

Mix flour and powdered sugar. Cut in butter. Press in bottom of 9x13 pan. Bake at 350 degrees for 15 minutes. Meanwhile, mix eggs (high speed) for 3 minutes, until pale and thick. Gradually add sugar and continue to beat one minute longer or until thick. Stir in lemon juice. Pour over "hot" crust. Bake an additional 15 to 20 minutes. Sprinkle with 2 Tbsp. powdered sugar. Cool.

Lemon Chess Pie
Jennifer Passmore

2 cups of sugar
1 Tbsp. flour
1 Tbsp. cornmeal
1/2 tsp. salt
4 eggs
1/4 cup butter, melted
1/4 cup milk
2 Tbsp. lemon juice
1/4 tsp. lemon extract
1/8 tsp. vanilla extract
Ready-made pie crust

This is a very old southern recipe. My mom made this for me every year for my birthday instead of a birthday cake, because I loved it so much! Crack 4 eggs and beat in a small bowl. Stir together sugar, flour, cornmeal and salt. Add eggs to the dry mix and stir. Add butter, milk, lemon juice, lemon extract and vanilla extract. Pour into a pie crust and bake on 375 for 35-45 minutes.

Lynd Fruit Farms Apple Pie
Aileen Freeman

Pastry for 2-crust pie
1/2 cup flour
1 tsp. cinnamon
6 cups sliced, tart apples (I use Granny Smith)
2 Tbsp. sugar
3/4 cup sugar
1/4 tsp. nutmeg
2 Tbsp. butter

Stir dry ingredients together. Add apples. Put all mix into pie pan. Dot with butter; seal with the top crust. Cut slits in top crust; then sprinkle the two teaspoons of sugar on top of the crust. Cover the edge of the pie pan with strips of aluminum foil. Remove the foil the last ten minutes of baking. Bake 40-50 minutes, until crust is browned and the juice starts to bubble through the crust.

Megan's Favorite Caramel Cake
Betsy Hall

1 German Chocolate cake mix or favorite chocolate cake mix
1/2 stick margarine
1 can sweetened condensed milk
20 caramel squares
Cool Whip

Make and bake cake as directed on the box, bake in a 9x13 pan. Cool for 10 min. While baking melt 1/2 stick margarine in small pan. Add 1 can of sweetened condensed milk (I use low fat). Unwrap 20 caramel squares. Add both to the melted butter and stir, watch so it does not burn. Punch holes in cake with the end of the beater. Pour over cake. Put in refrigerator. When cold put one carton of low fat Cool Whip on top of cake. Crush any favorite candy bar (Heath, or other) on top or I shave chocolate on the top. ENJOY and Blessings to you!!!

Lemon Sponge Pie
Kate Schau

1 cup sugar
2 egg yolks
Juice and rind of 1 lemon
Pinch salt
Pie crust

Butter the size of an egg
2 egg whites
3 Tbsp. flour
1 cup milk

Cream sugar and butter. Add egg yolks, lemon juice and rind, then flour and milk. Last, fold in beaten egg whites. Pour into unbaked 8 or 9 inch pie shell and bake in moderate 350 degree oven for 45-50 minutes. Cool to room temperature before eating.

Microwave Fool-Proof Fudge
Stacy Metz

32 oz. confectioners sugar
1/2 cup milk 1 cup butter
1 1/2 cups chopped pecans/nuts (optional)

1 cup unsweetened cocoa
2 Tbsp. vanilla

Mix sugar and cocoa in large glass bowl. Add milk and butter. (Do NOT stir.) Cook on high for 4 1/2 - 6 minutes or until butter is melted. Add vanilla and nuts and stir until smooth. Spread into sprayed 12x8 dish. Chill until firm. Cut into squares and serve. VARIATIONS: Rocky Road--add 1 cup mini marshmallows.

Mick's Chocolate Icing (Dad's)
Betsy Hall

(1/2 recipe is plenty)
1 box of confectionary's sugar
2 squares chocolate.
1 tsp. lemon juice
1/4 cup sweet cream
1 egg white (unbeaten)
2 Tbsp. warm water
Lump butter

Beat ingredients together at low speed. This recipe is very old-so I think chocolate was probably unsweetened. In memory of my dad...James B. Clover, Sr. Miss you!

Millionaire Pie
Eda Medina

This recipe is for four pies
4 ready made graham pie crusts
3 cans sliced peaches
3 cans pineapple tidbits
2 regular size whipped cream
1 can of condensed milk it has to be "La Lechera" brand
1 bag of pecans
4-5 drops of concentrate lemon

Drain the juice from both the pineapple and peaches. Cut the peaches into small pieces. In a big bowl add the fruit, whipped cream, milk and pecans. Once everything is mixed together add 4-5 drops of the lemon. Fill your pie crusts cover them and leave them overnight in the refrigerator. Ready to eat next day. Enjoy. (Please Do NOT use "La Lechera" that has the carmel taste –buy the regular flavor.)

Nilla Dippers
Sandy Taylor

1 box Nabisco Nilla Wafers
1 cup (or more) peanut butter, smooth or crunchy
6 squares Baker's Semi-Sweet Baking Chocolate

Divide entire box of Nilla Wafers in half. Spread 1 tsp. peanut butter on the flat side of half of the cookies. Top with remaining halves to make cookie sandwich. Microwave chocolate squares on high until melted, about 2 minutes. If not melted, continue to heat in 30 second intervals. Stir until smooth. Dip each cookie sandwich halfway into the melted chocolate, then place on waxed paper on a cookie sheet. Refrigerate 10 minutes or until chocolate is set. Makes about 40 cookies.

Oatmeal Bake
Pam Herrington

3 cup quick cooking oats
2 tsp. baking powder
1 tsp. salt
1/2 cup melted butter
2 eggs beaten

1 cup brown sugar
2 tsp. cinnamon
1 tsp. vanilla
1 cup milk

Combine all ingredients in order listed. Pour ingredients into greased 9x13 pan. Bake at 350 for 40-45 minutes.

No Guilt Apple Pie
Georgie Mygrant

2 tsp. of lemon juice
3 1/2 to 4 cups of coarsely chopped apples
Sprinkle lemon juice over apples and toss gently and set aside.

1 cup of whole wheat flour
1 cup of baking Splenda (or sugar if you like)
2 tsp. of baking powder
Mix last three together in a large bowl
5 egg whites, slightly beaten (or 1 cup of egg beater whites)
1/2 tsp. of vanilla
1/2 tsp. of walnut extract (or 1 tsp. of either one)
1/2 to 3/4 cup of chopped walnuts or pecans
Mix last 4 together with the flour mixture. Mixture will be thick. FOLD in the apples.

Transfer mixture into a LARGE pie plate, that been sprayed with non-stick spray. Bake at 350 for 45 minutes, until apples are tender and the top is golden brown. Let cool, then serve with sugar free cool whip or fat free ice cream. Without the nuts, this pie is fat free, but the nuts give it more flavor. You can switch the apples with peaches, cherries, blueberries, or rhubarb. Each time you make this pie, you'll be able to alter it to your liking. This way, you can have your pie, and eat it too! Enjoy!

Oatmeal Cookies
Marilyn Downer

1 1/4 cup margarine or butter
1/2 cup sugar
1 tsp. almond flavoring
1 tsp. salt
1 1/2 cups flour
3 cups oatmeal
3/4 cup brown sugar
1 egg
1 tsp. baking soda
1 tsp. cinnamon
1/4 tsp. nutmeg

Optional: 1 - 2 cups chocolate chips, raisins, or craisins

Mix butter/margarine, sugars, egg and almond together. Add dry ingredients. Mix well. Add chips or raisins. Bake 375 degrees for 8 to 10 minutes.

Only Because I Love You Pumpkin Spice Bars
Mindy Cress

2 cups all purpose flour
2 tsp. baking powder
1 tsp cinnamon
1/2 tsp. salt
1 cup oil
4 eggs
2 cups sugar
1 tsp. baking soda
1 tsp. ground nutmeg
1/2 tsp. ground cloves
2 cups canned pumpkin

Icing: Canned cream cheese icing

Preheat oven to 350 degrees. Grease 9x13 baking pan. In large bowl combine all ingredients, until moistened and "no" bumps are left. Pour in prepared pan and bake for 20 to 25 minutes until springy to the touch. Cool all the way and spread icing on top. Sprinkle with more cinnamon and serve at room temperature. P.S. You are only getting this recipe because "I Love You". God Bless!

Ooey Gooey Cake
Angie Martin

1 box white or yellow cake mix (not with pudding in the mix)
1 softened stick of butter
4 eggs
2 tsp. vanilla
1 8 oz. cream cheese
1 box powdered sugar

Mix together 1 box white or yellow cake mix, 1 soften stick of butter, 2 eggs, 2 tsp. vanilla, press in 9x13 pan or glass dish. Then mix 1 8 oz. cream cheese, 2 eggs, and 1 box powdered sugar. Beat together 5 minutes. Pour over white or yellow cake mix mixture. Bake at 350 degrees for 40 minutes. Let sit to cool 15 minutes approx and then cut into squares.

Orange Cookies
Jean Metz & Stacy Metz

Cookies:
2 cups sugar	1 cup shortening
1/2 tsp. salt	1 tsp. soda
1 cup milk	2 tsp. baking powder
2 eggs	4 cups all-purpose flour

Juice & rind of one large orange or 2 small ones.

Icing:
1 box 10XX confectioners sugar	1 tsp. orange extract
3/4 cup butter or margarine (melted)	1/2 cup milk

Cookies:
Cream together the sugar and shortening in mixer. Add eggs and beat well. Slowly add the salt, soda, baking powder, flour and add alternately with the milk into the cookie dough. Drop cookies by Tbsp. on greased cookie sheet. Bake at 375 degrees for 10 - 15 minutes.
Icing:
Stir together all ingredients and pour over cooled cookies.

Peach Cobbler
Shea Haupt

3 cups sliced peaches
1 stick butter
3/4 cup milk
Cinnamon to taste

1/2-1 cup sugar (if needed)
1 cup self rising flour
1 cup sugar

Preheat oven to 350. Melt butter in casserole dish in oven. Stir first sugar into fruit, if needed, set aside (use less or no sugar for more sweet fruit). Mix flour, milk, and cup of sugar for batter. Remove dish from oven and pour in batter. Spoon in fruit but do not stir. Bake for 45 min. or until crust is brown. Serve warm with ice cream! Note: I like to add fresh blueberries in with the peaches.

Peanut Brittle
Brenda Bakos

1 cup white sugar
1 cup white corn syrup
2 cups raw peanuts
1 heaping Tbsp. baking soda

Mix sugar and syrup and cook in heavy pan, stirring until it starts to boil. When the candy thermometer reaches 250 degrees, add peanuts. Continue cooking and stirring until it reaches 300 degrees. Remove from heat, and stir in soda. Pour onto greased baking sheet. Cool and break into pieces. Store in airtight container.

Peanut Butter Bon-Bons
Lorraine DelValle/Stacy Metz

1 can vanilla frosting-ready to spread
1 cup smooth peanut butter
1/4 cup softened butter
2 1/2 cups graham cracker crumbs
1 package vanilla, almond or chocolate bark

In a large bowl-combine frosting, peanut butter and butter. Blend well. Add cracker crumbs and blend well. Form 1 inch balls. Place in freezer for 15 minutes. Melt bark in microwave per instructions on package. Dip balls and place on wax paper until dry. Approx. 1 hour. If mixture seems wet or soupy add more graham crackers.

Peanut Butter Pie
Ernie McFarland

One 9 inch baked pie crust
1 cup powdered sugar
2/3 cup white sugar
2 cup milk
2 Tbsp. butter
3 Tbsp. peanut butter
1/2 cup chunky peanut butter
1/4 cup cornstarch
1/4 tsp. salt
3 egg yolks
1/2 tsp. vanilla

Blend 1/2 cup peanut butter and 1 cup powdered sugar. Take 1/2 mixture and place in bottom of pie crust. Combine remaining ingredients and cook in double boiler until thick. Stir constantly. Pour in pie crust. When cool add Cool Whip and put remainder of peanut butter and powdered sugar mixture on top.

Peanut Butter Pie
Lynn Francisco (in memory of Pam Smith)

2 pie crusts (cook crusts)
1 cup powdered sugar
1/4 cup crunchy peanut butter (or more)
1 large and 1 small box of instant vanilla pudding
Large Cool Whip

Mix powered sugar and peanut butter in bowl with fork 1/4 cup crumbly mixture set aside to mix with Cool Whip make pudding with 3 cups of milk Divide crumble mixture into 2 pie crusts. Spread and pour pudding on top. Then put Cool Whip mixture on top. Refrigerate over night.

Peanut Butter Pie
Janice Sprowles

1 8 oz. pkg. cream cheese, softened
1 8 oz. container whipped topping
1 graham cracker pie crust
1/2 cup peanut butter
1 cup powdered sugar
1/4 cup fudge dessert topping

Beat cream cheese and peanut butter until well blended. Gradually add powdered sugar and mix well. Fold in whipped topping. Spoon into pie crust and drizzle fudge topping over pie. Swirl knife through cream cheese mixture for marble effect. Refrigerate until firm.

Peanut Butter Finger Bars
Linda Rehder

1 cup butter or margarine (2 sticks)
1 cup brown sugar
2/3 cup peanut butter (creamy or chunky)
1 tsp. salt
2 cups flour

1 cup sugar
1 ½ tsp. baking soda
2 eggs
1 tsp. vanilla
2 cups quick oatmeal

Topping:
12 oz. pkg. of semi-sweet chocolate chips
1½ cups powdered sugar
6 - 8 Tbsp. milk or Half and Half

1/2 cup peanut butter

In mixing bowl cream butter, sugar, brown sugar, and eggs. Beat well. Add: baking soda, eggs, peanut butter, salt, vanilla and flour. Beat well. Last add oatmeal and beat until well mixed. Spread mixture in well greased 9x13 jelly roll pan. Bake at 350 degrees 20-25 minutes or until golden in color and toothpick comes out clean from center of baked bars. Immediately upon removing from oven, sprinkle chocolate chips on hot bars. Let sit so chocolate chips melt while you mix the following in a mixing bowl: powdered sugar, peanut butter and milk. Add enough milk until mixture is smooth and stirs easily. Do not leave mixture too thick. Spread this mixture over melted chocolate chips, swirling the chips and powdered sugar mixture together. Let cool completely before cutting.

Pineapple-Orange Sunshine Cake
Pam Herrington

Cake:
1 box yellow cake mix
1/4 cup applesauce
1 can (11 oz.) mandarin oranges in light syrup

Frosting:
1 container (8 oz.) light whipped topping, thawed
1 pkg. (3.4 oz.) instant vanilla pudding mix
1 can (15 1/2 oz.) crushed pineapple in juice

For the cake: Preheat oven to 350. In a large bowl, stir together all cake ingredients until moist. Beat by hand for two minutes. Coat 9 x13 cake pan with nonstick spray. Pour batter into pan. Bake 30-40 minutes or until toothpick comes out clean. Cool completely. For the frosting: In a large bowl, mix together all frosting ingredients until well blended. Spread over cake. Store in refrigerator. Serves 16

Pumpkin Cake
Lynn Francisco

1 yellow cake mix
1/2 cup oil
1 cup pumpkin
4 large eggs

3/4 cup sugar
1/4 cup water
1 tsp. ground cinnamon

Preheat oven to 350. Grease Bundt pan, 9x13 or 2 9" round pans. Mix all ingredients. Then beat until well blended. Bake 45 minutes

Pumpkin Cake Roll
Pam Herrington

3 eggs
2/3 cup pumpkin
3/4 cup flour
1 tsp. cinnamon
1/2 tsp. nutmeg
1 cup nuts

1 cup sugar
1 tsp. lemon juice
1 tsp. soda
1 tsp. ginger
1/2 tsp. salt

Cream Cheese Mixture:
1 Cup powdered sugar
4 tsp. butter

1 (8 oz.) pkg. cream cheese
1/2 tsp. vanilla

Beat eggs 5 minutes (not less); gradually add sugar while still beating. Stir in pumpkin and lemon juice. Stir together dry ingredients; stir into pumpkin mixture. spread on greased 15 x 10 x 1 inch pan. bale at 375 for 15 minutes. Turn onto a towel, sprinkled with powdered sugar. Start @ narrow end and roll towel and cake together; let stand. Unwrap and spread with cream cheese mixture. Reroll and refrigerate. Slice roll when firm.

Puppy Chow
Reba Pearson

1 pkg. chocolate chips
1/4 cup vegetable oil
1/4 cup creamy peanut butter
6 cups Crispex cereal
2 cups powdered sugar

Combine chocolate chips, oil and peanut butter. Microwave until melted. Pour Crispex cereal in a Ziploc baggie, add melted chocolate into baggie. Shake bag until cereal is well covered. Add powdered sugar and shake again, pour into bowl, cover and refrigerate for 1 hour or until cool.

Pumpkin Cheesecake
Jodi Faaborg

Crust:
1 3/4 cups graham cracker crumbs
3 Tbsp. light brown sugar
1/2 tsp. ground cinnamon
1 stick melted salted butter

Filling:
3 (8 oz.) packages cream cheese, at room temperature
1 (15 oz.) can pureed pumpkin
3 eggs plus 1 egg yolk
1/4 cup sour cream
1 1/2 cups sugar
1/2 tsp. ground cinnamon
1/8 teaspoon fresh ground nutmeg
1/8 tsp. ground cloves
2 Tbsp. all-purpose flour
1 tsp. vanilla extract
Redi Whip topping (if desired)

Preheat oven to 350 degrees. In medium bowl, combine crumbs, sugar and cinnamon. Add melted butter. Press down flat into 9-inch spring form pan. Set aside.

Beat cream cheese until smooth. Add pumpkin puree, eggs, egg yolk, sour cream, sugar and the spices. Add flour and vanilla. Beat together until well combined. Pour into crust. Spread out evenly and place oven for 1 hour. Remove from the oven and let sit for 15 minutes. Cover with plastic wrap and refrigerate for 4 hours. Top with whip topping of your choice and smile with every bite!!!

Pumpkin Sheet Cake
Stacy Metz

Cake:
1 can pumpkin (16 oz.)
1 cup vegetable oil
2 cups all-purpose flour
1 tsp. ground cinnamon
2 cups sugar
4 eggs, lightly beaten
2 tsp. baking soda
1/2 tsp. salt

Frosting:
1 pkg. cream cheese, softened (3 oz.)
5 Tbsp. butter or margarine, softened
3 - 4 tsp. milk
1 tsp. vanilla extract
1 3/4 cup confectioner's sugar
chopped nuts (if desired)

Cake:
In a mixing bowl beat pumpkin, sugar, and oil. Add eggs and mix well. Combine flour, baking soda, cinnamon & salt; add to pumpkin mixture and beat until well blended. Pour into a greased 15x10x1 inch baking pan. Bake at 350 degrees for 25-30 minutes or until cake tests done. Let cool.

Frosting:
Beat cream cheese, butter and vanilla in a mixing bowl until smooth. Gradually add sugar and mix well. Add milk until frosting reaches desired spreading consistency. Frost cake. Sprinkle with nuts.

Pumpkin Pie Cake
Melanie Richards

1 box yellow cake mix
4 eggs
1 (29 oz.) can pumpkin
1/4 cup soft oleo
1 cup chopped walnuts

1/2 cup melted oleo
2/3 cup milk
1/2 cup sugar
2 tsp. cinnamon
1/2 cup brown sugar

Set aside 1 cup of dry cake mix. Set oven at 350 degrees. Stir together remaining cake mix, 1/2 cup melted oleo, and 1 egg. Press in 9x13x2 inch pan. Mix together pumpkin, 3 eggs, brown sugar, cinnamon and milk. Pour over mixture in pan. Mix sugar (may be omitted if too sweet to taste), 1/4 cup oleo, and 1 cup cake mix. Crumble over pumpkin mixture. Sprinkle 1 cup chopped walnuts on top and bake 1 hour or until brown on top.

Quick and Easy Banana Cake
Peggy Butz

1 box yellow cake mix
2 eggs
1 cup sour milk
(1 cup milk, 1 1/2 tsp. baking soda, 1 Tbsp. cider vinegar)
3 ripe bananas crushed
Nuts, if desired

Mix all ingredients well; bake at 350 for 35-40 minutes. Top with favorite frosting.

Raw Apple Cobbler
Sue Powell

Filling:
6 apples, cored
2 tsp. cinnamon
1 tsp. vanilla
2 Tbsp. flaxseed, ground fine

1/2 tsp. sea salt
5 Medjool dates, pitted
1 cup raisins

Topping:
1 cup pecans
1 tsp. sea salt
2 tsp. cinnamon

1 cup walnuts
1 tsp. vanilla
5 Medjool dates, pitted

Soak dates in water for about 1 hour.

Filling: Place 3 apples, salt, cinnamon, dates, and vanilla in food processor. Process until mixture is almost the consistency of applesauce. Place mixture in a bowl. Chop the three remaining apples into small pieces in processor. Mix all of the apples together and add raisins. The raisins will soak up the juice from the apples. Stir in flax seeds and mix well. Let mixture sit at room temperature for 1/2 hour. Place apple cobbler in a pan and add topping.

Topping: Add salt, cinnamon, pecans & walnuts in a food processor and pulse the processor until ground. Add dates and vanilla and process until the mixture is processed well. Crumble this mixture over the top of the cobbler. Refrigerate.

Rocky Road Rice Krispie Treats
Shea Haupt

2 pkg. chocolate chips
1 pkg. mini marshmallows
2 cups chopped walnuts or pecans
1 pkg. white chocolate chips
4-5 cups Rice Krispies

Spray or butter a 9x13 glass dish. Melt chocolate chips in microwave. Remove and add marshmallows, Rice Krispies and nuts. Pour mix into dish and spread and then let set.

Rich Cherry Bars
Linda Rehder

1 cup butter or margarine
4 eggs
3 cups flour
1/2 tsp. salt
1/4 cup powdered sugar
1¾ cup sugar
1 tsp. vanilla
1½ tsp. baking powder
1 can cherry pie filling

Cream together: butter and sugar, add one egg at a time. Add: vanilla, baking powder, salt and flour. Mix thoroughly. Save out 1 ½ cups of batter for top of bars. Spread remaining batter in well greased 9x13 jelly roll pan. Spread pie filling over bottom layer of dough. In small amounts at a time, drop remain batter on top of pie filling. Bake at 350 degrees for 45 minutes or until toothpick comes out of center without sticking to toothpick. Sift powdered sugar over bars when you take out of oven. Cool before cutting.

Ritz Pie -- Mock Apple Pie
Lorraine Del Valle & Stacy Metz

Pastry for two crust 9-inch pie
1 Stack Pack Ritz Crackers
2 tsp. cream of tartar
Grated rind of one lemon
Cinnamon

2 cups water
2 cups sugar
2 Tbsp. lemon juice
Butter or margarine

Roll out bottom crust of pastry and fit into 9-inch pie plate. Break Ritz crackers coarsely into pastry-lined plate. Combine water, sugar and cream of tartar in saucepan; boil gently for 15 minutes. Add lemon juice and rind. Cool. Pour syrup over crackers, dot generously with butter or margarine and sprinkle with cinnamon. Cover with top crust. Trim and flute edges together. Cut slits in top crust to let steam escape. Bake in a hot oven at 425 degrees for 30 - 35 minutes, until crust is crisp and golden. Serve warm. Makes 6 to 8 servings.

Santa's Snickers Brand Surprises
Pam Herrington

2 sticks butter (softened)
1 cup light brown sugar
2 eggs
3 1/2 cups all purpose flour
1/2 tsp. salt
1 pkg. (13 oz.) Snickers Brand Miniatures

1 cup creamy peanut butter
1 cup sugar
1 tsp. vanilla
1 tsp. baking soda

Combine butter, peanut butter and sugars using a mixer on a medium to low speed until light and fluffy. Slowly add eggs and vanilla until thoroughly combined. Then mix in flour, salt and baking soda. Cover and chill for 2-3 hours. Unwrap all Snickers miniatures. Remove dough from refrigerator and divide into 1 tbsp pieces and flatten. Place a Snicker miniature in the center of each piece of dough. Form the dough into a ball around the Snickers. Place on a greased cookie sheet and bake at 325 for 10-12 minutes. Let cookies cool on a baking rack or wax paper.

Shoo Fly Cake
Liz Collins

4 cups flour
2 cups margarine
1 cup molasses

2 cups sugar
2 cups hot water
1 tsp. baking soda

Blend Together: flour, sugar, margarine (save 1 cup to scatter on top) Mix: water, molasses, baking soda. Add to ingredients in #1. Pour in 9x13 pan. Bake at 350 for 45 minutes.

Snowman Treat
Pam Herrington

1/2 to 3/4 cup creamy peanut butter
34 round butter flavored crackers
12 oz. white candy coating - coarsely chopped
34 miniature chocolate chips
9 pieces candy corn, cut lengthwise in half
34 milk chocolate M&M's
Assorted colors of decorating gel

Spread peanut butter over half of the crackers. Top with remaining crackers to make sandwiches. In a microwave - melt candy coating, stir until smooth. Dip sandwiches in chocolate; allow excess to drop off. Place on waxed paper. Immediately position chocolate chips for eyes and mouths and add candy corn half for the nose. Place an M&M on either side of face for ear muffs - connected with a strip of decorating gel. Let stand for 30 minutes until sets. Yields 17 servings.

Snickerdoodles
Lois C. Corl/Sydney Yoder

1 cup butter (no substitutes)
2 eggs
2 tsp. cream of tartar
1/4 tsp. salt
2 Tbsp. sugar

1 1/2 cups sugar
2 3/4 cups sifted flour
1 tsp. soda
1 tsp. vanilla
2 tsp. cinnamon

Preheat oven to 400 degrees. Beat well until sugar is dissolved: sugar butter, eggs. Add: vanilla. Sift together and stir in: flour, cream of tartar, soda, salt. Mix together cinnamon and sugar in shallow bowl and set aside. Roll into balls the size of small walnuts. (Refrigerating dough first will make this easier) Roll in cinnamon and sugar mixture. Place 2 inches apart on ungreased baking sheet. Bake until lightly browned but still soft to the touch. (These cookies puff up at first and then flatten out. They crisp up after they cool) Bake time 8 to 10 minutes. This dough makes a great base for many types of cookies. I usually double the recipe when I make it. Instead of rolling the dough in cinnamon and sugar, you can roll it in colored sugar, sprinkles, etc. I also like to add Nestle's melted chocolate to 1/2 the dough to make chocolate cookies. I usually put a walnut or pecan on top. You can also add flavorings, etc. My mom (Lois'), Lois Ruff Chambers, was soooo creative and a great cook! This was her recipe. She taught me to improvise recipes to make them better. Using all butter instead of margarine or 1/2 butter and 1/2 margarine or shortening, makes these cookies really crisp and much better in my estimation. Also, you can store all the variations together in the same container without fear of them getting soggy. They also freeze really well.

Sour Cream Raisin Bars
Linda Rehder

1 cup melted butter or margarine (2 sticks)
1 tsp. baking soda
1 3/4 cups flour

1 cup brown sugar
1 tsp. salt
1 3/4 cups Quick Oatmeal

Filling:
4 egg yolks
3 heaping Tbsp. cornstarch
2 cups sour cream (16 oz. container)
2 cups raisins

1½ cups sugar
1 tsp. cinnamon
1/4 tsp. cloves

In mixing bowl stir together: butter, brown sugar, baking soda, salt, flour and oatmeal. Pat ¾ of mixture in well greased 9x13 jelly roll pan (reserving ¼ of mixture for top of bars). In double boiler combine: egg yolks, sugar, cornstarch, cinnamon, cloves, sour cream and raisins. Stirring almost constantly. Cook mixture until thickened. Pour cooked mixture over batter in jelly roll pan. In small amounts, dot remaining batter over filling. Bake at 350 degrees for 20 minutes or until golden brown. Cool before cutting.

White Chocolate Cheesecake
Marge Wise

4 oz. fat-free cream cheese
1 cup skim milk
1 small box sugar-free white chocolate instant pudding
1 1/2 cups lite Cool-whip
1 reduced-fat graham cracker pie crust

Mix 4 oz. fat-free cream cheese with 1/4 cup skim milk. Whisk until smooth. Add 1 small box sugar-free white chocolate instant pudding and 3/4 cup skim milk. Whisk for one minute. Stir in 1 1/2 cups lite Cool Whip. Blend until smooth. Pour into reduced fat graham cracker pie crust. Refrigerate for 4 hours. Cut into 8 pieces.

South in Your Mouth Peach Cobbler
Angie Martin

1 12 oz. can sliced peaches not drained (can used spiced if desired)
1 cup sugar
1/2 or 1 cup self rising flour
(depends on your liking of thickness. I prefer 1 cup)
1 stick of butter melted
2 eggs
1 cup milk (whole or 2%)
1 tsp. vanilla
Dash of salt (optional)
Dash, two, or three of cinnamon, if desired

In mixing bowl, mix together flour, sugar and salt. Add milk, vanilla, and cinnamon (just a dash of cinnamon). Pour in 9x13 or deeper casserole dish. Pour peaches over mixture. (I cut peaches in half). Fold in mixture gently into peaches. Dash cinnamon on top for taste and decorate. Bake for 45 minutes to an hour (depending on oven) at 375 degrees.

Winter Pumpkin Pie
Sandy Taylor

1 9-inch deep dish pie crust, baked
1/2 cup packed brown sugar
1/2 tsp. ground cinnamon
1/4 tsp. ground nutmeg
1 quart vanilla ice cream, softened
Whipped cream
Walnut halves
1 cup pumpkin puree
1/2 tsp. salt
1/2 tsp. ground ginger

Combine pumpkin, brown sugar, salt and spices with a rotary beater. Blend in ice cream. Pour into pie shell. Freeze until firm. Serve frozen, garnished with whipped cream and walnut halves. Note: You may have extra pumpkin mixture than the pie shell can hold. Freeze extra in individual ramekins for a treat later!

Yum Yums
Pam Herrington

1 box Club crackers
2 sticks butter or margarine
1 cup white sugar
1 1/3 cup peanut butter
2 cups graham cracker crumbs
1 1/2 cups brown sugar
2/3 cup milk
2 cups (12 oz. pkg.) milk chocolate chips

Lay out crackers on deepest cookie sheet. Mix crumbs, butter, brown sugar, white sugar and milk. Melt down on low heat. Over med. heat bring to a boil exactly 5 minutes stirring often, When 5 minutes is up pour over crackers and spread evenly. Put another layer of crackers on top of caramel mixture, cutting edges to fit. Melt chocolate chips and peanut butter in small pan until just blended. Spread over cracker mixture and put in refrigerator to cool. Cut in desired squares. Makes 5 dozen cracker size pieces.

Zucchini Brownies
Terri Henson

2 cups zucchini grated
1/4 cups sugar
1 1/2 tsp. soda
1 tsp. vanilla
1 egg, beaten
Chocolate bark or chocolate frosting
2 cups flour
1/2 cup cocoa
Dash of salt
1 cup oil
1/2 cup nuts

Mix dry ingredients. Add zucchini. Mix well. Add 1 cup oil, 1 beaten egg, 1/2 cup nuts. Mix well. Pour into 11x14 pan. Bake in 350 oven 15-18 minutes. Frost with melted chocolate bark or chocolate frosting. Who would think brownies could be healthy!!!

Healthy Fare

"At the end of the ten days they looked healthier and better nourished than any of the young men who ate the royal food. So the guard took away their choice food and wine they were to drink and gave them vegetables instead."

Daniel 1:15-16

Healthy Fare

Baked Oatmeal
Licia White

3 cups Quaker Oats
1 cup brown sugar or 1/2 cup brown sugar splenda
1 cup milk
2 eggs
2 tsp. baking powder
1 tsp. cinnamon
2 tsp. vanilla
1/4 cup melted butter
1/4 cup applesauce
Dash of salt

In large bowl mix oats, brown sugar, cinnamon, baking powder, salt. Beat in milk, eggs, butter, applesauce, and vanilla. (optional- dried fruit to stir in) Pour in 8x8 or 9x9 casserole. Bake at 375 degrees about 30 minutes edges will be golden brown when done. Cut in squares and serve with a little warm milk poured over top and fresh berries if desired. Wrap individually and take one to work with you. Very healthy.

Banana Muffin (vegan)
Brian Hall Family

3 ripe bananas
1 cup sugar or agave
1 tsp. baking soda
1/4 oil or grapeseed oil
1 tsp. (or less) salt
2 cups flour (or spelt)

Put wet ingredients blend together; then dry (1 cup flour at a time) Spray muffin tins. Makes 12 muffins. Bake at 360 for 20-25 min.

Black Bean and Rice Burritos
Sue Powell

1/4 cup water
1 tsp. olive oil
1 onion, diced
1 bell pepper (red, orange, yellow, or green) seeded and diced
1 Tbsp. ground cumin
2 cloves garlic, crushed
1 tsp. black pepper
3 cups drained canned or cooked black beans
2 ripe tomatoes, chopped
1/2 cup salsa
3 cups cooked brown rice
Salt, to taste
Tabasco sauce, to taste
12 whole grain tortillas

Heat water and oil in a large saucepan. When hot, add onion and sauté until limp. Add bell peppers, cumin, garlic and black pepper and cook and stir 2 minutes longer. Add a little more water if necessary to prevent sticking. Stir in black beans, tomatoes and salsa and cook and stir for about 10 minutes. Add rice and season to taste with salt and/or Tabasco sauce. Serve on warm tortillas. Serve with salsa and/or guacamole.

Low-fat Pumpkin Pie
Beth Barnett

1 cup low-fat milk
1 large container of instant vanilla pudding
1 cup of canned pumpkin
1 container of fat-free Cool Whip
1 Tbsp. cinnamon
1 Tbsp. ginger
1 tsp. nutmeg

Mix low-fat milk and pudding together. Mix the rest of the ingredients together in separate bowl and add to the pudding mixture. Pour into graham cracker crust. Add some more Cool Whip on top, if desired. So easy and yummy!!!

Low-Fat Zucchini Fries
Coley Mays, Student Minister

Canola oil cooking spray
1/2 cup all-purpose flour
1 tsp. salt
1/2 cup whole wheat flour
2 Tbsp. cornmeal
1/2 tsp.-1 tsp. pepper
3 medium zucchinis cut into 1/2-inch-by-3-inch sticks
2 egg whites, lightly beaten

Preheat oven to 475 degrees. Coat large baking sheet with cooking spray. Combine flours, cornmeal, salt, and pepper. Dip zucchini pieces in egg whites and coat with the flour mixtures. Place the zucchini on the baking sheet. Coat all exposed sides with cooking spray. Bake on the center rack for 7 minutes. Turn the zucchini and coat any floury spots with cooking spray. Continue to bake until golden and just tender, about 5 more minutes.

Maddy's Savory Slaw
Erilda Waters

1/2 red cabbage, shredded
1/2 green cabbage, shredded
2 granny smith apples, peeled and chopped
3/4 cup raisins
1/2 cup sunflower seeds
1/4 cup red wine vinegar
1 3/4 cup Vegenaise
1 tsp. dry mustard
1 tsp. sea salt
1/2 cup chopped pecans
1/4 cup honey
1/2-1 cup red onion, chopped (optional)

Use food processor to shred cabbage and apples. Mix ingredients well and chill. Better the next day.

Not-Tuna
Erilda Waters

1 can organic garbanzo beans
1/4 cup sweet onion, chopped
1 Tbsp. nutritional yeast
1/8 tsp paprika

1/4 cup celery, chopped
3-4 Tbsp. Vegenaise
1 Tbsp. lemon juice
Sea Salt to taste

1 can organic garbanzo beans, rinsed & drained, then coarsely chopped in food processor Transfer to bowl and mix in the following ingredients: 1/4 cup celery, chopped 1/4 cup sweet onion, chopped 3-4 Tbsp Vegenaise 1 Tbsp nutritional yeast 1 Tbsp lemon juice 1/8 tsp paprika Sea Salt to taste.

Mango Chicken Skewers
Coley Mays

1 tsp. lime rind, grated
2 Tbsp. vegetable oil
2 tsp. chili powder
1/4 tsp. cayenne pepper
3 boneless, skinless chicken breasts
1 sweet red pepper
1 small red or sweet onion, cut into 1-inch chunks

1/4 cup lime juice
3 cloves garlic, minced
1/2 tsp. salt
2 tsp. honey
2 mangoes

In a small bowl, create marinade by whisking together lime rind and juice, oil, garlic, chili powder, salt, and cayenne pepper. Cut chicken into 1-inch cubes and place in separate bowl. Pour half of the marinade over top, toss to coat, and let stand for 20 minutes. Stir honey into remaining marinades and set aside. (Better yet, cover and refrigerate separately for up to 4 hours.) Meanwhile, cut off mango flesh from each side of pit. Cut in a grid pattern of 3/4-inch squares in flesh of each side down to (but not through) the skin. Gently push skin to turn inside out, and cut off the flesh. Chop any flesh left on pit. Core, seed, and cut red pepper into 3/4-inch pieces. Alternately thread mango, pepper, onion, and chicken pieces onto each of the 8 skewers. Brush with half of the reserved honey marinade. Discard marinade used for chicken. Place kabobs on a lightly greased grill over medium-high heat; close lid and grill, turning and basting chicken once with remaining honey marinade until fruit is softened and chicken is no longer pink inside (about 8 minutes).

Pumpkin Muffins (vegan)
Brian Hall Family

1 can pumpkin (small can)
1 tsp. cinnamon
1/2 tsp. clove
1 tsp. baking soda

2 cups flour
1/2 tsp. nutmeg
1/4 oil
1 cup sugar or agave

Wet ingredients first, blend. Then dry, 1 cup of flour at a time. Grease muffin pan. Makes 12. Bake at 360 for 20 min. - 25 min. (keep an eye on them)

Veggie Burgers
Diana Burnside

2 cans beans (black, pinto, great northern, any kind of bean would work)
1 cup shredded carrots
1/2 cup bell pepper, chopped
1/2 cup onion, chopped
2 cloves garlic, minced

1 stalk celery, minced
1/2 cup oatmeal (quick or old-fashioned)
Squirt of mustard
Squirt of ketchup

Sauté onions, garlic, peppers, and celery in 1 Tbsp. of olive oil. Set aside. Smash beans in big bowl. Add cooled sautéed mixture and oatmeal. Squirt mustard and ketchup. Form into 6 balls. Smash into patties. Freeze. When you want to eat one, put frozen patty into a pan with a couple of squirts of Pam. Spray one squirt on top of frozen patty. Over medium heat, fry patty 4-5 min. Spray spatula with Pam, turn, fry 4-5 minutes. ENJOY!

Blueberry-You're a Peach Jacki Decker!- Crisp
Lois Corl

1 quart blueberries (fresh fruit works best)
2 or more large peaches diced
Juice of 1/2 lemon sugar to taste
1/4 cup flour
1/4 cup oats
1/2 cup dark brown sugar
1/2 teaspoon cinnamon
Dash nutmeg dash salt
1/4 cup plus 2 tablespoons unsalted butter
1/2 to 1 cup walnuts broken or whole

Preheat oven to 375 degrees Combine blueberries and peaches in shallow baking dish. (9X13 or slightly smaller) Toss gently with lemon juice and a little bit of sugar to taste. Set aside. In a bowl, mix flour, oats, brown sugar, cinnamon, nutmeg and salt. Whisk together so that it is well blended. Melt butter and pour over oat mixture, toss well to form crisp. Add walnuts, toss. Drop in spoonfuls over fruit. Cook uncovered for 40 minutes. Enjoy!!!!

www.ingramcontent.com/pod-product-compliance
Lightning Source LLC
Chambersburg PA
CBHW071312110426
42743CB00042B/1281